# POWERBOATING

## A Guide to Sportsboat Handling

**Peter White**

**Fernhurst Books**

First published in 1991 by Fernhurst Books, Duke's Path,
High Street, Arundel, West Sussex BN18 9AJ

Printed and bound in Great Britain

British Library Cataloguing in Publication Data
White, Peter
    Powerboating
    1. Powerboats
    I. Title
    623.8231

    ISBN 0-906754-59-3

**Author's acknowledgements**

This book is a tribute to my many former students, whose constant
questioning highlighted the need for it. I would also like to extend my
thanks to Tim Goodhead (RYA Coach) who assisted with the rescue
photographs; Bas Messenger for his advice on the maintenance and
repair of rubber boats; Bill Mitchell for sharing his expertise on
outboard engines; Robin Nichols (BWSF) for supplying information on
ski boats; and Melanie Waite for so willingly and ably becoming a
student for the photographic sessions. Special thanks are also due to
Fletcher Boats  Narwahl (UK) Ltd and Zodiac (UK) Ltd for the loan of
boats, and Crewsaver for providing lifejackets for the photographs.

The publisher gratefully acknowledges the assistance provided by
the Royal Yachting Association in the different stages of the production
of this book, from concept to publication.

Dedicated to my wife, Hilary Claire. The book was her idea, and her
drive and enthusiasm have steered me through the whole project.

**Photographs**

All photographs by John Woodward, with the exception of the
following:
*Motor Boat & Yachting* magazine: page 5, 94
*Sports Boat* magazine: page 4, 6, 9, 11, 33, 69, cover (Chris Boiling)
Peter White: page 30, 70, 77


Edited and designed by John Woodward
Composition by Central Southern Typesetters, Eastbourne
Printed by Hillman Printers (Frome) Ltd, Somerset

# Contents

# Introduction

Powerboating is fun. The sensation of speed as you skim across the water in a fast planing boat is terrific, and the sun, spray and sea air combine to make it an unforgettable experience. You'll want to go out again and again, and maybe even buy a boat of your own. You may want to use it for waterskiing, as a dive boat or simply for transport across a big lake or between islands. You may need a safety boat for your sailing club or diving school. You may just enjoy zooming around. But either way, you'll need to know what you are doing.

In most parts of the world you do not need a certificate of competence to use a boat. You can just climb in and go. But with more boats on the water the frequency of accidents is increasing and many people are calling for restrictions. Before long you may have to pass a test before you can take your boat out. This is already law in some countries.

A lot of people object to the idea of legislation, for a variety of reasons, but the only sure way to avoid it is to make it unnecessary. If all boat owners knew how to handle their craft properly there would be no need for restrictions. Boating is also much more enjoyable if you are confident about your abilities on the water: you can try new techniques, get away from the crowds and explore new areas.

If you follow the advice and practise all the exercises in this book you will be well on the way to becoming a skilled boat handler. You should have no difficulty getting a certificate of competence if you need one. But more to the point, you will find that your powerboating is what you hoped it would be – fun.

# 1 What boat?

The first step towards enjoyable, safe powerboating is choosing the right boat. You probably have some idea of the type of boat you want, but whatever you choose it must be safe and suitable for the conditions of the water it will be used on. Some boats are designed for flat water, while others are specifically designed for coastal waters and open seas.

If you are going to use the boat for pleasure, then it must be fun and easy to handle for two people. If it is to be used for commercial purposes, it must be functional and safe.

## A BOAT FOR YOUR NEEDS

Before deciding on a specific boat, ask yourself these questions:

### What is it designed for?

Powerboats are used for a wide range of activities, including water skiing, parascending, ferry work, fishing, diving, club rescue, professional rescue, towing or simply as runabouts.

➤ **Choose your boat with care: a small sportsboat like this will make a great runabout, but will not be stable enough to be used as a fishing or diving boat.**

### Where will I use it?

Where you live and the type of water that you have access to should also influence your choice of boat. Powerboats are used in such diverse waters as inland lakes, ponds, rivers, reservoirs, flooded gravel pits, estuaries, coastal waters and on the open sea.

### Where will I keep it?

You can store a boat outside the house, in the driveway, in a garage, in a shed, in a boat park or a marina. When you are reviewing the options, give consideration to the problem of adequate security. Most insurance companies make stringent security stipulations.

### How often will I use it?

To ensure maximum usage of your boat, give careful consideration to all the above points. Many boats spend most of their lives on moorings or in storage because it is impractical to use them more frequently, or the wrong boat has been chosen for the activity pursued by the owner.

### Who is it for?

If you are to be the 'skipper' of the family boat, not only will you have to choose one wisely, but your responsibility will extend to maintaining it. This

includes arranging adequate insurance cover, buying suitable clothing and boat equipment, and making appropriate preparations every time you take the boat out.

If you use the boat commercially, it is vital to have a regular maintenance programme. Once again, the responsibility for this usually falls on one person.

## TYPE OF HULL

The nature of the hull will determine how a powerboat performs in various types of water, and at different speeds. This in turn influences its suitability for the activities you have in mind.

### Displacement craft

Displacement craft sit in the water and their speed is governed by the waterline length of the hull. They generally handle well and have good directional stability forwards, but going astern creates very heavy pressure on the rudder and steering is very difficult. Many such boats will travel in only one direction astern, because of the paddlewheel effect of the rotating propeller.

The speed of displacement craft is not unduly affected by the weight of the load, although they should not be overloaded. Their construction is usually robust and they will handle heavy weather quite well. Balance and trim are not of vital importance. They generally have inboard engines, and are left on moorings.

### Planing craft

A high-speed planing craft relies upon a large power unit installed in a properly-designed hull to push it from displacement mode up onto the plane. As the power increases, the hull is forced to ride the bow wave. With even more power the bow wave moves back towards the stern of the craft, so there is less hull in contact with the water and less resistance. As the boat flattens out on the water the speed increases and the engine can be throttled back.

► **A typical planing hull has a deep 'V' at the bow which gets progressively flatter towards the stern. Such a hull will plane over the water while cutting through wavecrests for a reasonably soft ride.**

Maximum speed depends on the shape and weight of the hull, engine, fuel, equipment and crew, as well as the wave height and wind strength.

A flat hull travels faster than a deep 'V'-hull, because the 'V' cuts through the water whereas the flat hull skims across the surface. However, a flat hull can only use flat water. If it rides waves, it will shake itself and the crew to pieces.

The best compromise is a hull with a deep 'V' at the bow, but becoming flat towards the stern. The deep 'V' parts the water at the bow and directs this water towards the flat area at the stern, which skims over the surface. The angle of the 'V' and the rate of flattening towards the stern varies from hull to hull depending on the conditions it is designed for, and it is important to choose the best design for the waters you will be using.

You will have heard the term 'dead rise' or 'flare'. The dead rise refers to the angle between the hull and a horizontal line drawn through a cross-section of the keel.

A conventional high-speed planing hull relies upon a dead rise at the bow of approximately 45° diminishing to an angle of 15° to 22° at the stern. This combination cuts through the waves and provides a reasonably soft ride. The main lift point occurs around the longitudinal centre of gravity, so the most critical factor affecting the planing performance of the boat is the angle of the hull aft of this central point.

Marine architects are constantly testing and developing different types of hull which do not necessarily conform to the accepted pattern in an attempt to increase speed and efficiency, and some of these are now in common use.

### Cathedral hulls and dories

These are designed for planing in moderate conditions and are ideal for sheltered waters. They are favoured by sailing clubs because they are often double-skinned with built-in buoyancy, enabling them to stay operational even when swamped. They make ideal platforms for carrying heavy loads, and are excellent workboats. They have good directional steering at slow speeds but can be very uncomfortable when travelling fast in large waves. Nevertheless, some of the more recently designed large dories will tolerate heavy conditions and are able to carry large payloads at very high speed.

### V-hulls

A V-hull craft has poor stability when at rest, but this improves dramatically when the boat is moving fast through the waves. A deep 'V' gives a soft ride because it cuts through the lumpy water. The shallower the 'V', the harder and less comfortable the ride.

Buoyancy is built into some craft. If not, some buoyancy should be put in for safety.

If the hull is long enough, you can choose between an outboard or inboard engine. Performance craft are often fitted with outdrives. Good balance and trim are essential.

### Semi-rigid inflatables

These combine the benefits of rigid high speed hulls and inflatable side tanks, offering speed plus soft contact with other boats, or people in the water. This makes them excellent rescue craft as well as fun boats. They possess a massive amount of buoyancy and can carry heavy loads, although balance and trim are essential to good performance. Their seaworthiness is excellent in heavy weather although the crew can become very wet. Many have self-draining cockpits.

Single or twin outboard or inboard jet engines can be fitted to these boats, which are best used with trailers or launching trolleys, although they can be left on moorings.

◀ **A dory (top) makes an excellent workboat, combining a roomy layout with great stability and load-carrying capacity. A rigid-hulled inflatable (bottom) is better for rescue work in exposed waters, since it has tremendous buoyancy and stability and copes well with heavy weather.**

## Inflatables

Inflatables are all-rubber in construction. Some have separate inflatable sections for the hull which, when pressurised, performs in a similar manner to that of a semi-rigid inflatable. These are very fast, very wet boats, often with excellent directional stability at high speed. At slow speeds they are greatly affected by the wind.

Inflatables are capable of carrying heavy loads and are extremely buoyant. Again, trim and balance are essential for good handling.

They are usually fitted with an outboard engine or engines. Very few inflatables are left on moorings overnight and therefore need a trailer or trolley.

## Tenders

A small inflatable fitted with a small outboard bracket and engine makes an ideal tender for a larger craft. It is excellent for short rides between the shore and boat, and can be deflated and stowed in a bag easily and quickly, making a trolley unnecessary.

## SKI BOATS

If you want to use your boat for waterskiing you must make sure you buy something appropriate. You need speed, manoeuvrability and the right kind of seating, in a hull that will cope easily with the water you have access to.

There are specialist ski boats on the market, but these are generally aimed at a particular branch of the sport and may limit your scope. For most recreational waterskiing the best choice is a GRP sportsboat. If you intend to keep the boat on flat inland waters you could go for a dory-type hull, but such boats can be uncomfortable in waves. A better option is a deep-V which will cut through choppy water and give a reasonably soft ride.

It is possible to waterski behind a very small boat, but the practical minimum length for serious sport is about 3.6 metres (12 feet). The upper size limit should be about 7.3 metres (24 feet): anything larger will not be able to turn quickly enough. The best choice for family recreational skiing is about 4.8 metres (16 feet).

◆ A tiny tender like this hardly qualifies as a powerboat, but you still need to know how to use it.

Many specialist ski boats have mid-mounted inboard engines, but the more adaptable type of craft normally have two-stroke outboard engines. Choose an engine that will give you all the power you need when it is working at roughly three-quarters capacity: you will need between 85 and 140 hp. The engine must be able to push the boat up onto the plane within 10 seconds of starting from rest, and this will effectively rule out many larger craft. A speedometer is a useful accessory, since it will help you maintain a constant speed.

The internal layout is important. Obviously you need something to attach the ski rope to, and the best solution here is a pylon with an attachment point about a metre (three feet) above the waterline. But with the smallest craft this will affect the handling to a dangerous degree, and you may have to attach the rope low down on the transom. This is a good argument for buying a boat of reasonable size.

It is essential to have a seat facing backwards for the observer. Many sportsboats have

adaptable seats that can be re-configured or swivelled round; check for this.

You also need plenty of floorspace for gear, and seats for two or three passengers. Keep deck fittings to a minimum, since cleats and fairleads are only snags waiting to tear the wet suits of tired skiiers clambering aboard. A boarding platform at the stern is invaluable in this respect. Boarding the boat by stepping on the cavitation plate above the propeller is definitely not recommended.

### THE ENGINE

Most small sportsboats use outboard petrol (gasoline) engines. You can get diesel outboards, but they are more expensive and very much heavier for the same power.

For a larger boat you might choose an inboard engine. This may be a petrol (gasoline) engine – probably a marinised car or truck engine – or a diesel. Some have simple shaft drives with rudders for steering, but these are not recommended for general-purpose boats. Better by far is an outdrive: a propeller on a swivel

**◆ A proper ski boat is specially designed for the job. If waterskiing is your main interest, make sure you get a boat with the right specification.**

**◆ Choose your engine carefully and it will serve you well – as long as you maintain it properly.**

mounting which is used to steer the boat in the manner of a swivelling outboard. Really powerful craft may have twin engines, and this gives you extra flexibility when manoeuvring.

### A power unit for the job

Always have a large enough engine to cope with the task you have set it. A small engine will be used flat out nearly all the time whereas a larger one will be used at three-quarters of its maximum output. However, an outboard engine enjoys working hard and often. It dislikes being left under a damp cover for weeks and weeks without work. An engine that is well used and well maintained by a professional engineer will work for thousands of hours. If abused, it may destroy itself on day one.

## PROPELLER

Propellers are made from a variety of materials. Outboards and small sportsboats usually use aluminium propellers which are reasonably priced and very efficient. Used correctly, their life expectancy will match that of the engine.

The blades of a propeller can be destroyed in seconds if the engine is put into gear when its lower leg is sitting on shingle, rock, a wooden slipway or concrete. Even if it is not completely wrecked, the propeller can be put out of balance if a large piece is missing from one blade. Used at speed, it will cause vibration which may harm the engine and the gearbox.

If the damage is minimal, an aluminium propeller can be rebuilt, which is cheaper than replacing it. When repaired skilfully, the propeller can be as good as new.

## ROAD TRAILERS

Do use a trailer recommended by the manufacturer of the boat, designed or adapted to fit the boat concerned. It must offer maximum support to ensure safe trailing, launching and easy recovery from a variety of sites.

Small powerboats can safely be carried on two-wheel trailers, but depending on the weight of the boat, the size of the towing vehicle and the legal requirements of the country in which you are towing, the trailer may be required to have brakes. Heavy craft should be transported on braked, four-wheel trailers. Dealers and manufacturers can advise on the most suitable equipment.

The road trailer must be strong enough for the boat and maintained in good condition. It is costly, embarrassing and possibly very dangerous if a trailer collapses while it is being towed along the road.

Road trailers are often used for launching into deep, salt water which is very corrosive. Ideally, if you keep the boat on dry land close to the launching site, use a separate launching trolley. Your road trailer will last far longer.

### Break-back trailer

This is a trailer designed for launching and recovering a boat without immersing the wheel bearings in the water. The success of this depends on the skill of the person doing the job, coupled with the angle of the slope at the launching site. If the angle is too shallow, the boat will slide off the trailer and the transom will hit the ground. Break-back trailers take some getting used to, but they can be very effective in the right circumstances.

# 2 Getting afloat

A boat is no use without water to use it on, and it has to be the right type of water.

## Rivers

Many small rivers and canals are only suitable for sedate boating in low-speed displacement craft. The charm of such boating lies in the beauty of the surrounding countryside, and having the time to stop and appreciate it. This type of boating is very relaxing, but can involve numerous problems that are not immediately obvious. These include avoiding weirs and shallows, negotiating locks, overhanging trees, low bridges and cables, and keeping clear of shallow sections on the insides of bends. Most rivers and canals display speed limits and, on the whole, fast powerboats are not welcome unless they are just 'gurgling' along. Some larger rivers may have designated high-speed areas suitable for planing craft.

## Lakes

Inland lakes and gravel pits offer a totally different boating environment. Many are now being used for a combination of water activities, including jet biking, waterskiing and powerboat racing. For safety reasons, use of the water is generally tightly controlled, with a limited number of craft allowed on it at any given time. Users must stick to a specific circuit route, and club membership and training are necessary before going afloat.

## Reservoirs

Reservoirs are not really the domain of powerboat users. They are frequently used by sailing clubs and fishermen and often include sections set aside as nature reserves and bird sanctuaries. On the whole, the only powerboats allowed on reservoirs are those used for rescue services and by the water authority.

**◗ The flat water of an inland lake is ideal for waterskiing, but access is often restricted. Check this before you buy your boat, since the type of water may affect the type of boat you need.**

## Estuaries

Estuaries often look quiet and peaceful, owing to the shelter offered by the surrounding land, and they usually offer excellent sites for the launching and recovery of powerboats. However, you must always beware of the hidden dangers of estuaries.

Consult a chart to find the shallow areas where the flow of the river meets the open sea. Sand and mud are brought down the river and deposited in and over the entrance to an estuary, creating a 'bar'. Invariably there is only a narrow passage, navigable at certain states of the tide.

A tide rip will build up where different currents of water meet, often causing small whirlpools. Overfalls occur when a large body of moving water squeezes over a shallow area, creating a

turbulent race with short, choppy waves.
Sometimes a boat can only pass through such
waters at certain states of the tide.

### Coastal waters

A whole book could be devoted to this topic.
Basically there are some stretches of coastline
which are ideal for powerboating and other
stretches where it would be far too dangerous to
venture out. Yet it is not always obvious which is
which.

Local knowledge is essential. Ask yourself the
following questions: Do many people use this
stretch of coastline for sailing, windsurfing,
yachting, fishing or water skiing? Is it busy? Are
there any harbours where a boat can seek shelter
if the weather deteriorates? Do these harbours
offer refuelling facilities and good launching and
recovery facilities?

If you can answer 'yes' to these questions then
this is likely to be a suitable coast to explore with
your powerboat. But if the waves are pounding on
the shore and there is nobody in sight, then go
elsewhere.

➤ **A good launching site will offer all the facilities you
need for fuelling, launching and recovering the boat,
washing it down and parking it while you change and
get something to eat.**

### Offshore waters

You should only venture offshore in a small
powerboat if the conditions are ideal and the
weather forecast is favourable. Your boat must be
well equipped, you must plan the journey
carefully and never attempt it alone.

Yet despite all this a journey of over 100
nautical miles out of sight of land is not unrealistic
for a fast, powerful craft in the hands of a
competent crew.

## ACCESS TO WATER

There are three ways of getting access to the
water: obtaining permission to use a private site,
relying on public amenities or, on the coast,
launching off the open beach.

### Private launching sites

Some private sites are owned by individuals, but
most are the property of recognised clubs and
marinas. In most cases non-members can arrange
to use the launching and recovery area, but you
may have to join a club to gain access to other
facilities.

Some clubs let you handle your own launch and
recovery while others have their own equipment

with professional staff operating it. This equipment might consist of four-wheel drive vehicles, tractors or hydraulic lifting forks which are designed to lift a boat from the shore and lower it into the water alongside the pontoon. Recovery is effected in the same manner. One advantage of joining a club is that you can often store the boat on site, which saves trailing. When storage space is at a premium, sportsboats can be safely stacked in racks, one above the other.

All this costs money, of course, and you may find trailing the boat to a public site is a cheaper option.

### Public launching sites

As the name implies, these are for the use of the public, for launching and recovering any water-borne craft that are permitted within the local rules and regulations. This may include dinghies, powerboats, canoes, jet bikes and fishing boats.

There are public launching hards that are neglected, silted up and blocked with rubbish, but many are very well maintained and offer excellent facilities. You will have to pay a fee for the use of these facilities (payable either daily, weekly or annually) but it will probably work out cheaper than joining a club.

### Open beaches

Launching and recovering a powerboat on an open beach is possible, but often difficult. Success depends on several factors: the firmness of the shore, the slope of the beach and the available depth of water. If all these are suitable, you still have to give consideration to the wind strength and direction.

Large waves breaking on the shore indicate a strong onshore wind which makes launching the average sportsboat virtually impossible. Suitable rescue craft can be launched in these conditions, provided there are enough helpers, adequately clothed, but it is a tricky business (see Chapter 3).

Coastal clubs are equipped to deal with such problems, with concrete or wooden ramps, rubber rollers, rubber matting, plus hand or electric winches with cables or ropes to retrieve the boats. Since launching from an open beach can be risky or even dangerous, it is better to join a recognised powerboat club that can offer such facilities.

## LAUNCHING CONSIDERATIONS

An ideal launching site would offer:
- Reasonable access for vehicles and boats.
- Off-site parking for vehicles and trailers.
- Wide slipway.
- Strong construction (if of timber, check that it will take the weight of your vehicle).
- Not too steep an angle.
- Clean (free from seaweed and slime, so a person can stand on it without slipping).
- Sufficient water for launching and recovery at all states of the tide.
- Pontoons for mooring.
- If the site is tidal and dries out, a hard that will take the weight of trailer wheels.
- A winch.
- Fresh water available for washing down.
- Changing facilities and toilets nearby.
- Food available nearby.
- Fuel in the vicinity.
- Telephone.

## WEATHER CHECK

Make sure you obtain a weather forecast several hours before you go afloat on a large area of water.

The most important factor, apart from the obvious – sun or rain – is the strength and direction of the wind, since this will determine the state of the water. Strong winds build large waves, while the direction of the wind determines the nature and effect of the waves.

Strength is measured by the Beaufort Scale, while wind direction is defined by the source of the wind: a westerly gale blows from the west.

For large vessels at sea, Beaufort Force 8 is recognised as a gale, but gale warnings for small ships in inshore waters are broadcast whenever the wind strength is expected to reach Force 6 (20 knots). Inexperienced boat handlers should not take their boats out in winds greater than Force 4, since small boats may well be unsafe in winds of Force 5 and above.

Beaufort is measured at 33 feet above sea level (in clean air) so it is impossible to gauge wind

## WIND SPEEDS

| Beaufort force | General description | Speed (knots) |
|---|---|---|
| 0 | Calm | Under 1 |
| 1 | Light | 1–3 |
| 2 | Light | 4–6 |
| 3 | Light | 7–10 |
| 4 | Moderate | 11–16 |
| 5 | Fresh | 17–21 |
| 6 | Strong | 22–27 |
| 7 | Strong | 28–33 |
| 8 | Gale | 34–40 |
| 9 | Severe gale | 41–47 |
| 10 | Storm | 48–55 |
| 11 | Violent storm | 56–63 |
| 12 | Hurricane | 64 and over |

## SPEEDS OF WEATHER SYSTEMS

| | |
|---|---|
| Slowly | 0–15 knots |
| Steadily | 15–25 knots |
| Rather quickly | 25–35 |
| Rapidly | 35–45 knots |
| Very rapidly | Over 45 knots |

## TIMING OF GALE WARNINGS

| | |
|---|---|
| Imminent | within 6 hours |
| Soon | 6–12 hours |
| Later | 12–24 hours |

('Later' is also used about wind changes in forecasts)

strength by simply standing on the seashore and testing the wind against your face. Use a hand-held wind gauge and make the necessary adjustments to your recorded wind strengths (the wind loses its strength by approximately one-third at sea level because of the drag effect of the waves).

The same strength of wind will have an entirely different effect on the sea state if it is travelling with the tide or against it. For example, if a Force 4 wind is travelling with the tide, the sea will be fairly choppy. If a Force 4 wind is blowing against the tide, the sea will be very lumpy and could even be dangerous. The wind will try to prevent the movement of the water and it bumps up into steep waves.

The direction of the wind relative to the coast is also important. A near-gale blowing off the land may have little effect on the sea state, but the same wind blowing in from the sea will build up big, dangerous waves.

### The weather map

The weather maps used by forecasters are built up from measurements of atmospheric pressure: the weight of the air on the earth's surface. This pressure changes as the air temperature changes: warm air will rise and create a low-pressure area, while cold air will sink and create a high-pressure area. As the warm air rises, it allows the cold heavy air to rush in to balance out the pressure, and we experience this air movement as wind.

Gales occur when there is a large difference between the high-pressure area and the low-pressure area, and the low-pressure area draws in the surrounding cold, heavy air at high velocity. Low pressure areas are unstable with rain and wind, whereas high pressure areas enjoy more stable conditions.

### Sources of weather information

Information regarding the weather can be obtained from:

- Local and national television (weather forecasts are given at set times)
- National radio (weather forecasts are given at set times – gale warnings are given as and when needed)
- Marine weather services
- VHF Marine broadcasts
- VHF Marine radio (ship-ship and ship-shore)
- Local radio in coastal areas
- Telephone pre-recorded services
- Coastguard stations
- Harbourmasters
- Newspapers

So there is no excuse for not being aware of the weather which is predicted.

Remember that the wind direction and sea state can change within minutes, regardless of the forecast, so always keep an eye open for visual changes in the weather. When the wind increases and the sky begins to fill with very dark clouds, it is wise to be safe rather than sorry, and head for the shore.

## ESSENTIAL EQUIPMENT

### For small lakes
- Fire extinguishers
- Ropes
- Fenders (if necessary)
- Anchor chain and warp (rope)
- First aid kit
- Engine tool kit
- Spare fuel (if necessary)
- Radio (CB or Cellphone)
- Boathooks
- Knife
- Paddles
- Keys

### For coastal waters
Add the following to the above list:
- Compass
- Charts
- Flares
- Radio (VHF)
- Exposure blankets
- Plastic bin liner
- Fog horn
- Torch
- Mooring warps
- Fenders
- Food and hot drinks
- Spare propeller, and the tools to fit it

- Navigation lights
- Spare 2-stroke oil
- Spare spark plugs

### Equipment for the crew
Choose your clothing according to the climate and weather conditions, but remember that it is always very much colder over the water than on land. Use this as a checklist, and select what you need.
- Lifejacket or buoyancy aid (essential)
- Spare lifejackets
- Ski jacket
- Waterproof coveralls
- Boots/trainers
- Wet socks
- Dry suits
- Wet suits
- Steamers
- Thermal hats
- Gloves
- Thermal underwear
- Jumpers/sweaters/t-shirts/trousers
- Towels for necks
- Sunglasses (with retaining strap)
- Sun cream/lotion
- Sun hats
- Cool clothes for sun protection

▲ In some countries many items of essential equipment are legal requirements.

# 3 Launching and recovery

Before you consider launching your boat, check the weather forecast. Then check the wind direction and the effect it is having on the water. If the wind is blowing from the water onto the land and creating large waves, launching will not only be very difficult but may also be dangerous. If the wind is coming across the land and blowing out to sea, the sea will be quite flat. This is ideal for launching, but remember that the wind can change direction during the day. Conditions at 10 am might be fine, but if a windshift is predicted four hours later, it could make recovery very difficult by heaping up large breaking waves.

The other thing to check is the state of the tide. There are many tidal launching sites that dry out and can only be used for a few hours each side of high water. Marker posts indicating the height of water are generally situated close to the shore at such sites, and when the water level falls to a certain point all craft have to be removed from the water, otherwise they will run aground.

## LAUNCHING

Ideal conditions for launching would be no wind and no tide, and a slipway that allows the car to stay attached to the trailer throughout. Despite this the wheels of the car do not go anywhere near the water, and the wheel bearings on the trailer remain above the surface. The angle of the slipway and the depth of the water allow the craft to be slid off the trailer with a gentle push.

### Final preparations

1 Position the vehicle and boat out of the way of others using the slipway.
2 Remove the lighting board and electric cable from the trailer.
3 Remove the boat ties and the protective cover from the engine and boat.
4 Prepare the craft:
   - Complete the engine check, securing everything on board
   - Check fuel, oil (and water, if an inboard engine)
   - Check the fuel system and gears and ensure everything is ready to fire up
   - Check the hull for visible damage
   - Check the clothes of all crew and remember the lifejackets
   - Check the painter (rope) is attached to the bow. This is the most important rope on small boats.
   - Check all drain bungs are in place.

⬇ **A steep slip may allow you to launch the boat without unhitching the trailer, but on a shallow slip you will need to use a long rope.**

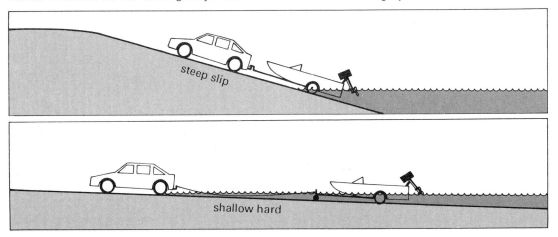

steep slip

shallow hard

5 Keep the trailer winch cable, or strop, attached to the boat until the craft is in the water. If you take this off and then move down a steep slipway, the boat will slide off the trailer onto the ground, damaging the hull.

6 One competent driver could be in the boat for the launch.

7 Ensure the engine is tilted up on the hydraulics or, if manual, locked in the up position.
If the engine is down when launching, serious damage could occur.

## The launch

1 Reverse the vehicle and boat towards the water, taking care not to submerge the wheels of the vehicle.

2 When the boat starts to float at the stern, stop the vehicle and secure the brakes.

3 Assuming the launch conditions are ideal, the driver on board can lower the engine into the water, ensuring that it does not touch the bottom. The engine does not need to be completely down, as long as the cooling water intake is below the waterline.

4 If you are the boat driver, follow the recommended start procedure and start the engine.

5 Immediately check that the cooling water is circulating through the engine. If not, close down the engine and refer to the section on 'Troubleshooting' in Chapter 12 (it takes a few seconds for the water to circulate).

6 Set the engine revolutions to roughly 1500 rpm and allow a three-minute warm-up. If this is skimped the engine is likely to stall when you engage gear, leaving the boat drifting around out of control.

7 With the engine happily ticking over in neutral, ask to be released from the winch cable.

8 Engage reverse gear and slowly go astern off the trailer. Pick up a mooring, anchor, or tie up to a jetty or pontoon.

9 The vehicle and trailer can now be removed from the slipway and parked safely above the high water mark

DO NOT OBSTRUCT THE SLIPWAY –
EMERGENCY VEHICLES MAY REQUIRE
ACCESS AT ANY TIME

⬆ **On a steep slip, back down until the boat is floating at the stern.**

⬆ **With the engine warmed up, ask to be released from the winch strop. The boat may need to be pushed clear.**

⬆ **Slowly go astern off the trailer, into deeper water.**

⬆ **When you are well clear of the shallows you can engage forward gear and motor off to pick up a mooring.**

## Wind and tide

In the real world, consideration has to be given to the variations in tide and wind and their combined effects. In practice, you should do all the final preparation as itemised above, and then pause.

- Look at the water. What is happening?
- Is the tide rising or falling?
- Is the wind stronger or weaker than the tide?
- Is the wind in the same direction as the tide, or against it?

Look at other boats, especially those at anchor or on moorings. Look at flags or smoke to assess the wind direction. If the tide is stronger than the wind, the boats on moorings will point into the tide. These are described as 'tide rode'. If the wind is stronger than the tide and coming from a different direction, moored boats could be pointing at the wind or at a point between the direction of the wind and tide. These are referred to as 'wind rode'. Deep-keeled sailing boats will be more influenced by tide than shallow-drafted motor boats.

It is important to be able to discern which is stronger – the wind or the tide – because your boat will drift sideways immediately it is released from its trailer. You must ensure you have sufficient room to manoeuvre and allow for the drift before your boat starts to move under its own power. Once you have planned a course of action, carry on with the launch procedure.

➤ **You can assess wind and tide by checking the wave direction and looking at moored boats. Deep-keeled yachts will generally point into the tide, while a shallow-drafted cabin cruiser will be blown by the wind. Work out what is happening and try to predict which way your boat will drift when you launch it.**

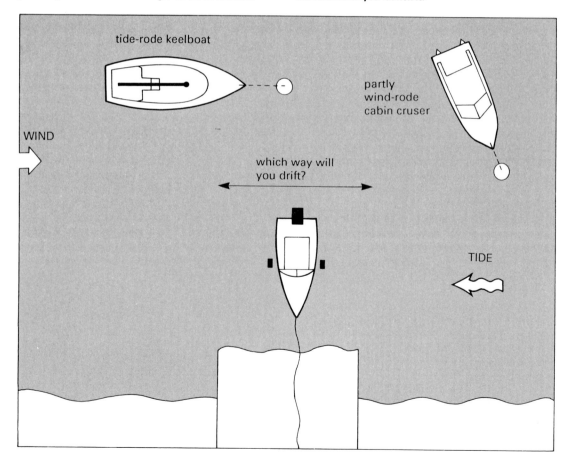

tide-rode keelboat

partly wind-rode cabin cruser

WIND

which way will you drift?

TIDE

## STARTING THE ENGINE

### Outboard

1 Check the mix of fuel and two-stroke oil.
2 Open the air vent on the fuel tank.
3 Prime the engine by squeezing the bulb in the fuel line until you feel a resistance. (Make sure the bulb is fitted so that the arrow points down the line towards the engine.)
4 Turn the choke control on, either manually (on a hand-pull engine) or by pushing the key, button or switch (electric start). Make sure the kill cord is fitted, or the engine will not (or should not) start.
5 Check that the gears are in neutral and open the override throttle.
6 With an electric start, fire up the engine by giving short bursts on the starter. With a hand-pull engine, make sure you are balanced and clear of other crew members and give a good solid pull on the cord.
7 The engine should have started by the third attempt. Immediately it fires, close the choke (or switch it off, if electric).
8 Adjust the throttle to roughly 1500 rpm and check that the cooling water is circulating.
9 Warm up the engine for three minutes.
10 Check that both forward and reverse gears are working before moving off.

### Inboard

1 Turn on the electrics at the isolation switch.
2 Switch on the air blower for five minutes.
3 Check that the fuel is on.
4 Isolate the gear lever from the gears.
5 Pump the gear/accelerator lever forward about three times to inject fuel into the carburettors.
6 Set the lever in fast tick-over position.
7 Start the engine by giving short bursts on the starter. If it fails to start on the third attempt something is wrong.
8 Check that all the dials and controls are working, and that the cooling water is circulating.
9 Warm up the engine for three minutes at the recommended warm-up speed.
10 While at tick-over, re-engage the gears and check forward and reverse before leaving the pontoon or mooring.

To stay in control after the boat is released from the trailer, try to go astern into the direction from which the wind or tide is coming. This will stop the boat being swept sideways: onto other craft, ashore or aground. Watch others and don't be tempted to copy their mistakes.

If the wind is really strong it can pile up big waves that may wash the boat straight off its trailer. Even larger waves will break right over the stern. If in any doubt, do not launch.

### Launching from a hard in shallow water

Hards are simply hard areas of shingle, strong enough to take a heavy vehicle without it sinking in. This only applies to the centre of the hard, though, for the movement of water across a shingle hard moves the stones off the centre to the edges, where they stick in the mud. The edges look hard but this is misleading and they should be avoided.

The slope of the hard is often variable, starting shallow and then falling away into deep water. Many hards can only be used at certain hours either side of high water.

At some launching hards the water is shallow for many metres before it becomes deep enough to launch a boat. If you follow the method given above, the water will come well over the door sills of your launch vehicle. The answer is to use a long rope, which has several advantages:

- It prevents the trailer disappearing.
- It can be used to recover the trailer after launching, and to recover boat and trailer at the end of the day.
- It keeps the vehicle dry.
- It reduces the risk of physical injury.

The technique of launching with the rope in shallow water is as follows:

1　Having made all final checks, reverse down the hard and stop the tow vehicle and trailer clear of the waterline.

2　Drop and secure the jockey wheel.

3　Attach the end of the long rope to the trailer, using a bowline knot. Loop the rope around the ball hitch on the tow vehicle.

4　While holding the rope, release the trailer from the ball hitch.

5　If the trailer has brakes, use the hand brake-lever to control the trailer as it rolls down the slip into the water. Meanwhile allow the rope to slip around the ball hitch on the tow vehicle.

6　If there are no brakes on the trailer, use the rope to control it as it rolls downhill. The ball hitch takes most of the strain so you should have no difficulty stopping the trailer, but take care not to release the rope or it may burn your hands.

7　When the boat starts to float at the stern, secure the rope to the tow vehicle using a clove hitch.

8　Wade out, release the boat from the winch cable/strop and gently push it off the trailer. Hold onto the painter (rope attached to the bow) and move the boat away from the trailer. The boat will swing round to point into the wind or tidal stream.

9　Meanwhile, someone else can retrieve the trailer by towing it out on the rope.

10　When the car driver returns, he or she can climb aboard while the other crew member holds the bow of the boat in the shallow water.

11　Use the paddles – NOT the engine – to move the boat into deeper water where you can pick up a mooring. Only use the engine if you are quite sure there is no danger of grounding the propeller.

　Never allow the boat to drift while you try to start the engine. If it is reluctant to start you could easily drift half a mile or more before you get under control, and if you have a mechanical problem you could soon be in serious trouble. Trying to paddle a sportsboat against the wind and/or tide to return to the hard is virtually impossible. Having launched the boat, tie it to a nearby jetty or mooring before turning your attention to the engine. If there is nothing to tie it to, consider using the anchor.

⏴ Tie the rope to the trailer using a bowline knot.

⏴ Loop the rope round the towing ball and unhitch the trailer.

⏴ Allow the trailer to roll down the slip, controlling it with the rope.

⏴ When the boat is floating, tie off the rope using a clove hitch.

☛ **If the water is deep enough you can motor off the trailer. Warm up the engine, release the strop (left) and reverse clear (centre). Get someone else to pull the trailer out of the water on the rope (right).**

## ROUGH WEATHER

It is useful to look at launching into waves from a shingle beach as there are those people who would need to do so. Coastal sailing clubs often have weekend sailing regattas and races in the most adverse conditions. Once clear of the breaking waves on a lee shore, sailing dinghies can handle winds above Force 6, provided they have experienced safety and rescue crews in attendance. The boats used for rescue would be displacement diesel craft, dory-style rescue boats or rigid inflatables which are kept ashore.

For this example, the rescue craft is a rigid inflatable with manual lift on the outboard engine and maybe a reinforced keel.

Shingle beaches are not good for trailers, since they tend to sink in and become stuck, so the boat has to be removed from the trailer and placed on large roller bags, gas pipes or rubber mats. You then manhandle it down to the water. Several pairs of hands are needed for this, plus two runners to take the roller bags from one end to the other.

It is best if the bow enters the water first, since it does not carry the weight of the engine and will lift as the waves come in. You then move the craft into deep water, keeping the bow in the waves while lowering and starting the engine. There is no time for a warm-up period, although the engine could be warmed up beforehand by using the muffs and a hose. Engage forward gear and take off into the waves, taking them on the bow.

The dangers and problems associated with this technique are clear:
- A wave hitting the bow just off-centre will swing the boat sideways.
- Helpers will have water above their waistlines, will become partially buoyant and lose their ability to stand and hold the boat.
- A large wave could send the boat sideways back to the shore, straight over the helpers. If the engine is down it could be damaged and waves will break on board and swamp the boat.
- To avoid injury, helpers must keep clear of the propeller as it moves away.
- The helm must have total command and be aware of everybody in the water.

Once away from the shore, the waves will be softer and more manageable, and once one craft is afloat, this can be used to tow others off the shore:

1 The launched boat holds station or anchors clear of breaking waves and sends a floating link back ashore. This should have a small float attached to it.
2 Connect this to the shore boat which already has its crew aboard, and is being held by helpers.
3 Once connected, push the boat out into the deeper water, signalling to the stand-off boat to pull away.
4 When you get into deeper water, lower the engine, fire up and cast off the tow line.

### Fixed rope method

An alternative method is to position a large mooring out to sea with a rope running along the seabed and back to the shore. This is fixed to the shore above the high water mark. You can use this rope to manhandle the boat out into deep water. This technique is safer and requires less people in the water.

When you return to the shore, pick up this mooring, switch off and lift the engine. Then, by using the rope, work your way back to the beach.

### Experienced crews only

A crew of three can launch a boat into breaking waves, but it requires a rare determination. For this example, the craft is a four-metre rigid inflatable.

1 Move the boat into the water, bow on. One person is aboard and prepared to start the engine. The other two are holding the boat, one each side, and quickly moving it into deep water.

2 The first breaking wave to strike the boat rides over the bow and begins to fill it up. Quickly move into the deeper water, lower the engine and fire up.

3 By this time, the second and third waves will have broken into the boat, rapidly filling it with water and weighing it down.

4 Quickly go into gear as the crew roll in, put the power on and drive into the next wave. The bow rises as the power comes on, causing the water to rush to the stern. Make sure it doesn't overwhelm the engine and swamp it. Drive through the next wave and into the clear water beyond the surf.

5 Open up the transom flaps or elephant trunking and empty the craft. You may need to use a bucket or bailer to speed up the process.

## RECOVERY

Returning home after a trip out can be confusing because the scene may be different: land that was covered with water earlier is now dry, or vice versa. If it is possible to come alongside a jetty or pontoon, do so and tie up there. This will allow you time to fetch the vehicle and trailer, and assess the situation.

It is not wise to leave a boat on the shore with a falling tide, since it could be high and dry by the time you return with the car and trailer from the car park. If there is no jetty, one person must remain with the craft, standing in the water and pushing it gently away from the drying shore.

A boat left on the shore with a rising tide can also create an amusing spectacle for onlookers. As the tide rises the boat will float off and away unless one member of the crew stays behind to hold onto it.

Whatever the state of the tide, you should always try to avoid beaching the boat, for the hull will swish about with the waves and could be damaged.

1 With the boat tied on the jetty, reverse the trailer close to the water and drop the jockey wheel. Attach the tow rope to the trailer with a bowline knot and release the trailer from the vehicle.

2 Push or lower the trailer into the water, deep enough to cover the stern runners.

3 Release the strop from the winch and pull it out to nearly the length of the trailer.

**Approach slowly, with the engine slightly raised.**

**With the boat on the trailer, get off and attach the strop.**

**Winch the boat right up onto the trailer.**

**4** Take the tow rope and connect it to the ball hitch, using a clove hitch. Leave some slack in case the trailer needs to be moved in deeper.

**5** Return to the boat and drive it slowly towards the trailer. Check the wind and tide direction, and aim to arrive slightly to one side of the trailer, so the boat tends to drift onto the trailer rather than off it. Approach very slowly.

**6** If the engine is on hydraulics, lift the engine just enough for the anti-cavitation plate to be seen, but do not lift it too far or the water cooling system will fail. Check the water jet for circulation.

**7** When you are getting close go into neutral, then switch off the engine and lift it fully. Climb over the bow into shallow water and hold the boat.

**8** Move the boat into position over the rear of the trailer and connect the strop. Go to the winch handle and swing the trailer to line up with the boat. Then winch the boat onto the trailer.

**9** A dry member of the crew can then start the vehicle and slowly retrieve the trailer and boat. Once on the flat, the vehicle can be reversed and hitched to the trailer.

Larger craft can sometimes be driven onto the trailer. This requires a very slow approach in calm conditions, and the trailer needs to be deep in the water. Two guide posts at the rear of the trailer are essential if you are using this method, since the trailer itself is submerged. The posts will also help to line up the approach and will keep the craft central on the trailer. Pipe insulation material wrapped around the posts will help prevent damage to the boat.

When the craft is on the trailer, go into neutral, switch off and lift up the engine or lower leg. Climb off over the bow, keeping clear of the trailer. Connect the strop and then signal the driver to slowly tow the boat out. As it starts to leave the water, check the trailer rollers are in position. If one has rolled out of position, then return the trailer to deeper water and reposition the roller by hand. But be careful not to trap your hand or fingers between the roller and the hull. Even small waves will lift and drop the hull, with potentially bone-crushing consequences.

If you are using a larger craft with a cross-wind or cross-tide, try to organise a long rope from the stern of the boat to a crew member ashore. This should prevent the stern from swinging away.

With larger, heavier craft, do not rely too heavily on the winch. Try to float the boat as close as possible to the winch itself. Be prepared to get wet and do allow a lot of time for the recovery of a heavy boat.

At some sites there are tractors on stand-by. On seeing you arrive, one drives down the slipway with your trailer. This makes life much easier. The tractor driver guides you and does the winching. He then pulls you up the slipway and you do not even get wet feet, although you may prefer to climb out and position the boat on the trailer yourself. Other places use the hydraulic lift. All you to do is leave the boat on the jetty and the rest is done for you.

▸ **Raise the engine fully if you have not already done so.**  ▸ **Tow the trailer and boat clear of the water on the rope.**  ▸ **Back up to hitch the trailer on properly.**

## LANDING IN HEAVY SEAS

Rescue craft launched from the beach in the surf often have to return to the beach in the same conditions. On lee shores the waves can be very powerful indeed, so the technique is fraught with danger. Understandably, this is often referred to as an emergency beaching. In this example the boat is a rigid inflatable with a manual-lift outboard engine.

1 While standing off in the waves, release the lock on the outboard engine and test it to see that the engine will in fact lift (this lock is only needed when going astern). Do not drop the engine back down, since it could relock. Gently position it down.

2 Depute someone to stay by the engine while you concentrate on steering through the waves and selecting the best moment to turn for the beach. You will need to accelerate to travel faster than the following wave towards the shore. If you travel too slowly, the wave will catch you up and either break over the stern or push the stern off course. Within seconds you will be side-on and in imminent danger of being rolled over.

3 Ignore what is happening behind you and aim for the beach on the plane. As you hit the shallows, cut the engine and shout 'lift!' to the crew so he lifts the engine as you hit the shore. Then you both jump out, keeping hold of the lifelines, and use the forward momentum to pull the craft forward and up the beach (if you're lucky). Take advantage of the waves to move the boat further ashore.

From this description it should be obvious that this is no place for the GRP lightweight sportsboat. Lee-shore beaching is serious stuff, and should only be attempted by an experienced crew in a powerful, sturdy boat.

## TAKING TO THE ROAD

Trailing the boat can be a worrying business as you wonder whether the straps will hold, whether something will come adrift or even fall off halfway home. It's worth taking the time to make everything secure.

1 Check that all the rollers and supports are correctly placed and the nuts are tight.

2 Grease the wheel hub bearings and try them for side movement. If they are loose, readjust them.

3 Tie down the bow from the D-ring to the trailer. Use adjustable ties or strops for securing the boat to the trailer. Make them tight. Pad them out with pieces of carpet where they make contact with the hull and tension them well.

4 If the boat has an outboard, lock it up on the locking lever and place the propeller bag over the lower leg of the engine. This is a legal requirement. Often the locking lever is not strong enough, so insert a block of wood onto it and lower the engine.

5 Attach the trailer lighting board, connect the plugs and check the lighting. Secure the lighting wire to keep it clear of the road.

6 Lift the jockey wheel and make it secure, well clear of the road. Clamp it hand-tight only; if you use your foot you may strip the thread.

7 Lock the trailer to the ball hitch on the vehicle if possible. Connect the automatic brake wire if fitted. If the trailer should break lose, this will automatically apply the brakes on the trailer. Check the tyre treads and pressures, visually at least.

8 Check and secure anything that is loose in the boat, as this could cause damage in transit. Be sure to secure the fuel tank and batteries.

9 Think twice about putting on the boat cover if you are going to be travelling at speed. The wind could tear it to pieces.

10 Walk around the whole rig and check it over from a distance, asking yourself whether you have missed anything.

### Essential check

Move out onto the open road and, after a few miles, find a place to stop. Re-check all the ties and the position of all rollers and supports.

# 4 Boat handling

You need to become familiar with your boat at low speed before you open up the throttle. The first step is getting to know the controls.

### Steering
There are two basic types of steering: tiller and steering wheel control. On boats with engines of up to 20 hp you will often find tiller-steering. Craft fitted with engines of over 20 hp normally have steering wheels to give better control.

### Gears and acceleration
Small engines are fitted with one forward and one reverse gear, controlled by one lever per engine. Always be positive when engaging gears from neutral. If you move the lever too slowly the gear teeth will jump, causing damage to the gearbox. Always return to neutral and pause awhile before changing gear.

Acceleration is controlled by the same lever. Once you have engaged gear you simply move the lever further forward or back to increase speed. All engines have a facility to disengage the gears when you need to warm up the engine.

### Kill switch
The boat should be fitted with a kill switch – a cord or wire which is clipped to the helmsman's wrist or leg at one end, and attached to a trip switch at the other. Pulling on the cord releases the switch which then flicks off, killing the engine. The advantage of this should be obvious: if the helmsman falls overboard the engine cuts out, and the boat stops. Without the kill switch the boat could well disappear over the horizon, leaving the helmsman helpless in the water.

There should always be at least two people in a sportsboat, but if the boat hits a steep wave it could easily eject the whole crew into the water. On the open sea the consequences could be fatal if the kill switch is not being used. Use it.

### Fuel tank
Many sportsboats have portable fuel tanks which need to be connected up to the fuel line. The

◄ Moving the gear lever gives you forward or reverse. The further you move it the faster you go.

◄ A secondary lever allows you to open the throttle in neutral for starting and warming up the engine.

◄ Always clip on to the kill switch.

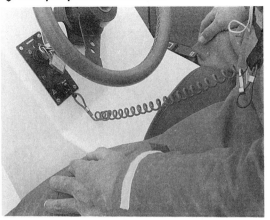

engine then has to be primed with fuel before it will start. With an outboard, always leave this until the engine is in the down position.

### Trim and balance (cargo and crew)

Correct trim and balance improves the performance of all powerboats. It is particularly important in small, fast planing craft but has less effect on heavy displacement boats.

Trim is altered by the fore-and-aft position of crew and cargo. If there is too much weight at the front of the boat the bow will dig into the water. If there is too much weight at the back, the boat will ride with the stern low and be difficult or impossible to bring up on the plane. Ideal trim varies from boat to boat, but if you concentrate the weight at the centre you will not go far wrong.

Balance is altered by side-to-side weight distribution. This is simpler than trim: if the boat is level all will be well. With two people in the boat the balance is usually fine, but a lone 17-stone driver sitting on one side of the boat will create an

➤ **Sit side by side to balance the boat. A pronounced list will do nothing for the handling.**

➤ **Fore-and-aft trim can have a dramatic effect on performance. With the weight too far back (left) the stern will ride low; too far forward (centre) and the bow digs in. With the weight central the boat will ride easily and fast.**

irregular hull contact with the water, causing speed and handling to suffer considerably. Since there should always be two people in a sportsboat this situation should never arise, but with three or more people you may have to give some thought to seating arrangements.

## BASIC MANOEUVRES

Driving a boat is not like driving a car. For one thing, you steer with the back rather than the front. This can be disconcerting at first, particularly when you are in a tight corner.

Even more alarming are the effects of wind and tide. A boat blown by the wind tends to slide sideways over a watery 'road' which is itself sliding to and fro over the ground. The combination of these two effects can be confusing, frustrating, expensive and sometimes dangerous, so you must learn to allow for them and even make use of them. The ability to use wind and tide constructively is one of the marks of a good boat handler.

### Gurgling speed

The best way to learn about boat handling is to practise a few basic manoeuvres at slow speed, with the boat simply gurgling through the water on minimum power. At this speed the boat creates hardly any bow or stern wave and uses very little fuel.

If you apply more power you create a lot more turbulence in the water and the engine uses more fuel, but the speed stays much the same. This is because you have reached displacement speed – the maximum speed at which the hull will travel while it is sitting in the water.

Getting up on the plane requires a lot more power to 'unstick' the boat – but once it is up there you can reduce the power, rather like accelerating hard in a car and throttling back to cruise at speed. A powerboat is efficient while it is either gurgling along or up on the plane; at any other speed it is wasting fuel.

### Figures-of-eight

Driving round a couple of buoys or moored boats at gurgling speed is an excellent way to learn about your boat. Choose two marks about six or eight boat-lengths apart and weave your way round them in forward gear. Notice the way the stern kicks out when you turn, and watch for the effects of wind and tide. You will probably have to compensate for these: a cross-tide or cross-wind will drive the boat to one side, while a tide that is flowing with or against you will change the rate at which the boat reacts to the helm.

Keep going until you can steer a steady course around the marks, then try the same route in reverse. If you find yourself travelling astern (backwards) into waves take care that they do not flood the engine or swamp the boat.

▶ **Manoeuvring around two buoys in a figure-of-eight will show up the steering characteristics of your boat and help you appreciate the effects of wind and tide. Go round the route both ways, and try it in reverse.**

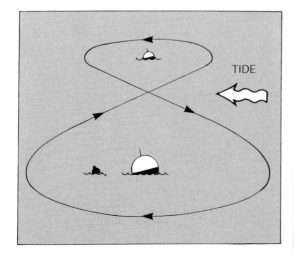

TIDE

⬆ **For a three-point turn,
first steer into the wind.**

⬆ **Go into neutral and swing
onto the other lock.**

⬆ **Engage reverse to pull the
stern round. The wind will help.**

### Three-point-turn (single engine)

In a harbour, marina or close to moored boats you
may find yourself in a position where you cannot
turn round in one movement. The only option is a
manoeuvre similar to that of a car turning in a
narrow road. Usually called a three-point-turn,
this may involve several forward and reverse
alterations of course, but the manoeuvre can be
greatly simplified by creative use of the wind and
tide. It is well worth practising.

1  Study the area in which you have to turn. Check
   the wind or tide and slowly start the forward
   turn on a hard lock into the wind and/or tide.
2  For this example, first turn to starboard (right).
   When you have turned as far as you can – and
   while keeping the lock hard on – move the
   gear lever to neutral.

3  As soon as you are in neutral, turn the lock hard
   to port (left). When you are on full lock engage
   reverse gear to pull the stern round.
4  Hold reverse and lock for a short distance, then
   move the gear lever to neutral.
5  As soon as you are in neutral turn hard to
   starboard, engage forward gear and drive off.
   You should be facing in the opposite direction.

   If you get this right you should have moved the
boat through a complete 180° turn in an area
equal to 2–3 boat lengths, or even less. The wind
or tide will help push the bow round (if you judge
it right) and the manoeuvre will be tightened up
considerably if you swing the wheel from lock to
lock while the boat is in neutral. The propeller
should always be facing the correct way before
you engage gear and accelerate away.

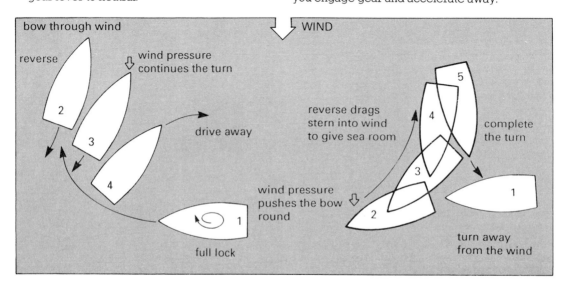

🔺 **Back in neutral, swing onto the other lock.**

🔺 **Engage forward gear to stop the boat.**

🔺 **Motor forward, back the way you came.**

If you need to turn a long boat in a very confined space you may be unable to turn the bow across the wind, and the boat will simply drift sideways. If you have this problem turn away from the wind in forward gear, then 'back up' into the wind in reverse. Go into neutral, swing hard over onto the other lock and hit forward gear to motor out in the opposite direction.

Practise these 180° turns in open water before trying them in a tight spot where you might hit something. A full 360° turn is also worth practising, since it involves both the techniques described.

### Three-point-turns (twin engines)

A boat with twin engines can be turned in just the same way, but by using one engine in forward gear and one in reverse you can get the boat to rotate in its own length without moving the steering.

### Manoeuvring in wind and tide

At low speed the wind and tide (whichever is stronger) will always tend to push the boat to one side or the other. As you become more skilled you can use this to manoeuvre the boat.

For example, try slipping sideways between two buoys while keeping your boat pointing more or less into a moderate current. When you come up alongside the starboard buoy, stay in forward

gear and adjust the throttle so you keep station. This is a useful exercise in itself. Then steer slightly to port, so that the current pushes along the starboard side of your hull. If you have the revs right you will glide across towards the port-hand buoy. Straighten up, and you should come gently alongside and keep station. Reverse the procedure and glide back the other way. Keep going until you've mastered it.

For your next trick, use the same technique to manoeuvre round a buoy, keeping the engine in forward gear and the boat pointing in roughly the same direction throughout. Slip sideways, increase revs to move forward, throttle back and slip across the other way, then throttle back further and glide back to your starting point.

Now try it in reverse.

🔹 You can achieve a tight three-point turn in a small boat by steering into the wind, which will help to spin the boat round. With a larger boat you may need to steer away from the wind initially.

🔹 When a boat is lying at an angle to the wind or tide the forces tend to push it sideways. You can use this effect when manoeuvring in a tight spot.

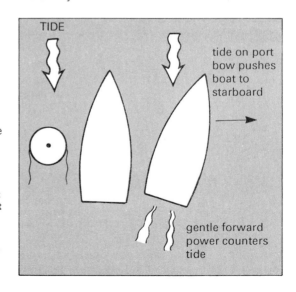

TIDE

tide on port bow pushes boat to starboard

gentle forward power counters tide

## INTERACTION

When you are manoeuvring in close proximity to moving vessels you need to be careful. Apart from the obvious danger of a straightforward collision, you must also beware of the effects of interaction.

If you have ever stood on a railway platform when a fast train roars through, you will know something about this. As the train arrives it pushes a pressure wave before it which blows your hat off, and as it passes it tends to suck things in towards it. This is why the station authorities tell you to stand back, well away from the edge of the platform.

The same thing happens with boats, but because water is denser than air the pressure waves are much more powerful. With a displacement craft they are also visible as bow and stern waves, while the dip in between is the suction zone. At this point, roughly amidships, water is actually being sucked under the hull – and if some unfortunate should fall overboard from a large vessel he may well be dragged under and ejected through the propellers at the stern.

This can have equally alarming consequences for nearby vessels. For example, the pressure wave created by the bow of a big boat moving at displacement speed extends well in front, and will tend to push everything else aside. If the big

▲ **At displacement speed this cruiser creates pronounced bow and stern waves. The dip between the two is the low-pressure or suction zone.**

vessel is overtaking a smaller boat the pressure wave may well push the small boat's stern aside, throwing it off course. With its engine still going, the small boat veers off at an angle to its original heading – straight across the bows of the overtaking vessel.

▼ **The bow wave from a large overtaking vessel will tend to push the stern of a small boat to one side – forcing the boat to steer straight across its path.**

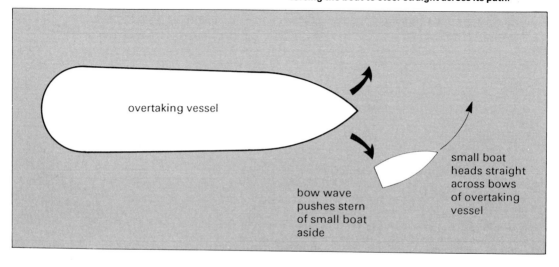

overtaking vessel

bow wave pushes stern of small boat aside

small boat heads straight across bows of overtaking vessel

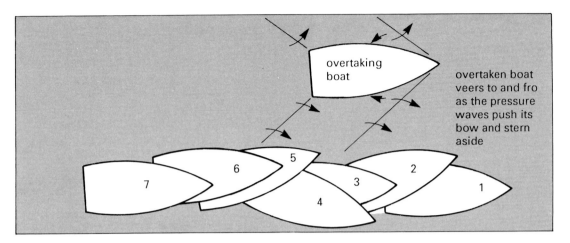

overtaking boat

overtaken boat veers to and fro as the pressure waves push its bow and stern aside

The message is clear: stay away from bigger ships, since they are surrounded by pressure waves that can destroy you. There may appear to be plenty of room, but don't be misled. Keep well away. With a large cargo ship travelling at speed, even a quarter of a mile may be too close.

Interaction will also affect two small boats. Each has pressure waves and suction zones, and when one passes too close to another there will come a point when both suction zones are adjacent. The boats are dragged together with alarming force.

Normally you would try to avoid this, but it can be useful. When operating two rescue craft at speed, experienced helmsmen can gradually bring them alongside 'shoulder to shoulder' and the pressure waves will hold them together. To

**◀ When you are overtaken by a vessel its pressure waves will cause you to veer about alarmingly, but if you keep the helm straight the forces will cancel each other out and you will stay on course.**

break away, both boats are gently throttled back and turned away from each other.

Interaction can even affect a solitary small boat if it is travelling at high speed in shallow water. At speed the hull forces the water apart and may 'vacuum' the hull onto the sea bed. This usually removes the engine, at the very least. Stay clear of shallow water, and if you can't stay clear, slow down.

**◀ By exploiting the suction zone you can hold two craft together at speed. To break away, throttle back and turn the boats away from each other.**

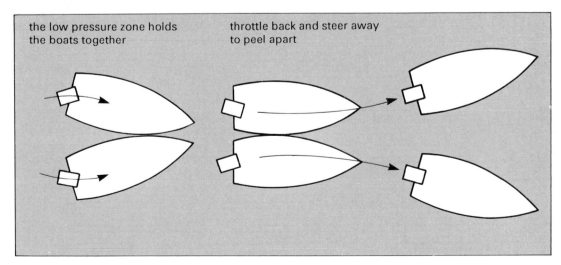

the low pressure zone holds the boats together

throttle back and steer away to peel apart

# 5 On the plane

Sooner or later you will want to open the throttle and take off on the plane. This can be really exhilarating – but you need to know what you are doing. Less obviously, the crew need to know too.

### Crew safety

Crew safety is partly a matter of being properly equipped, and partly a matter of knowing what is going on. Everyone should wear safety equipment, and everyone should be seated and secure whenever the boat is moving. In addition, everyone in the crew needs to be warned about any high-speed manoeuvres in advance, so they can prepare themselves and enjoy the experience. If you try to show off to your crew by flying across the waves and throwing them about without checking that they are properly prepared, they will end up shaken, frightened, and possibly injured. Remember that the speed across water appears to be about three times the speed over land. This has been compared to sitting in front of a video with everything rushing towards you and flashing past. If you're not used to it, this can be a pretty alarming experience.

As far as the driver is concerned, total concentration and vigilance are required at all times. An experienced helm moulds into the boat and becomes almost part of it, like a motorcyclist on his bike. He knows when to accelerate and when to close down; when to turn and when to power straight on. He is able to judge the size and speed of the waves at a glance, and detect the telltale signs of shallow water or floating hazards. But it takes hours and hours of practice to reach this level of competence. Don't fool yourself. Just because the brochure says that the craft will do fifty miles per hour, it does not mean that the driver can. Be cautious, and never drive beyond your limitations. You could break something, and it might be painful . . .

## GETTING UP ON THE PLANE

For your first high-speed run the sea needs to be reasonably flat, with little wind, plenty of sea room and well away from any speed restrictions. Ensure everyone is sitting comfortably and check that the kill switch is clipped on. Then, with one hand on the steering wheel and one on the throttle, tell the crew what you are going to do and wait for their acknowledgment.

➥ **From gurgling speed, check all is well and start increasing the power.**

➥ **The bows rise while the stern drops. Keep building the power to 'unstick' the boat.**

### Straight-line run

For a straight line run, gradually build the power on. The bow will rise while the stern drops, and the bow wave will start to move towards the stern. As the boat starts to climb the hump, keep building the power. The speed increases as the hull comes unstuck and the bow drops. As the boat levels out it starts to plane across the water.

Once on the plane the boat will try to race away, so you should reduce the power but maintain the plane. It takes a lot of energy to lift the boat, but once it is up there is much less water resistance on the hull, so you can throttle back to a comfortable speed for the conditions.

While you are on a straight-line run, throttle back a little and hold it there. The boat should slowly lose speed and come off the plane. The wave at the stern moves forward and becomes a bow wave again. Throttle back slowly until the boat stops and move the lever into neutral.

Repeat the exercise and watch the stern wave as the craft comes off the plane. As the apparent weight of the boat increases, so the stern wave increases in size. Remember that this stern wave is travelling at the same speed as the boat. By stopping slowly, the stern wave catches up with the boat slowly. If you throttle back from a planing mode instantly, the stern wave will surge up on you and possibly break over the stern, filling the boat with water and leaving you without an engine running. As the stern wave rides over the

▬ The boat climbs the bow wave and levels out on the plane. Throttle back to keep the speed under control.

▬ Throttle back slowly to come off the plane while staying ahead of the stern wave.

stern, it will also propel the boat several metres further forward.

A touch of forward throttle will move the boat away from the stern wave and prevent a swamping, but sooner or later you are going to have to stop quickly in an emergency. For this you need a special technique.

## EMERGENCY STOP

If you are up on the plane and an emergency arises, instantly reduce the power and, a second later, put the helm hard over to port or starboard. As the craft slides sideways – and stops – the sternwave will pass innocently to one side. The

◆ **If you throttle back instantly the stern wave will overtake you. It could easily swamp the boat or drown the engine, and will push the boat further forward – perhaps causing the collision you were trying to avoid.**

boat should stop within two or three boat lengths from the start of the manoeuvre.

Practise this procedure at several different speeds until you can accomplish it successfully when you are driving flat out. Different hulls and different weights will react in different ways, so you need to know your craft well.

◆ **By making a sharp turn immediately after shutting down the power you avoid the collision and avoid being overwhelmed by the stern wave, which carries on in a straight line. The diagram on the right shows the situation.**

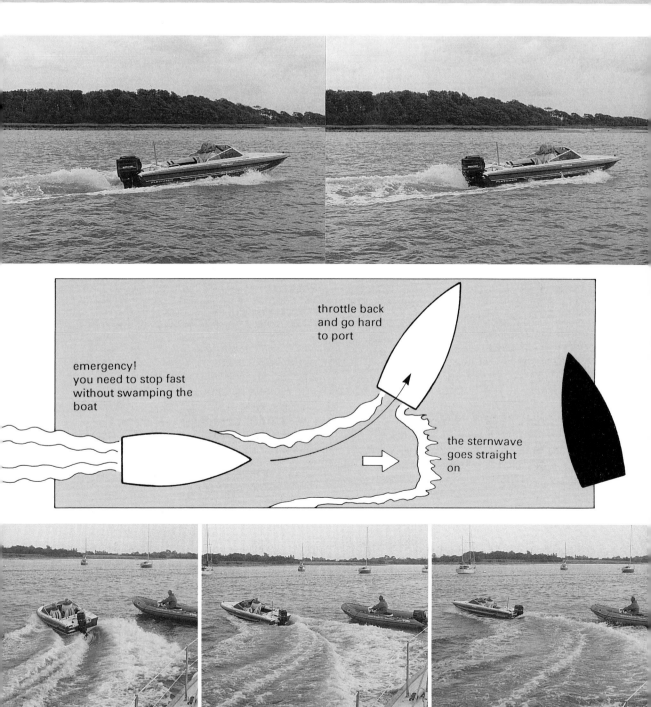

throttle back
and go hard
to port

emergency!
you need to stop fast
without swamping the
boat

the sternwave
goes straight
on

## TURNING AT SPEED

High-speed manoeuvres require a sensitive hand on the throttle and good crew communication. Always tell your crew what you are going to do, so they know which way the boat is going to turn. Remember that they do not have a steering wheel to hang on to.

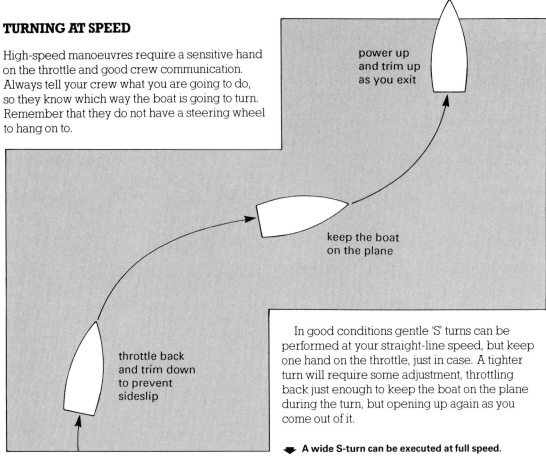

power up
and trim up
as you exit

keep the boat
on the plane

throttle back
and trim down
to prevent
sideslip

In good conditions gentle 'S' turns can be performed at your straight-line speed, but keep one hand on the throttle, just in case. A tighter turn will require some adjustment, throttling back just enough to keep the boat on the plane during the turn, but opening up again as you come out of it.

▶ **A wide S-turn can be executed at full speed.**

A 'U' turn is similar: a wide, gentle turn can be executed at speed, but a tighter turn involves some dexterity with the throttle. Having told your crew what you are about to do, throttle back until the boat is just planing and steer into the turn. As the speed drops because the hull does not like being pushed sideways, increase the power slightly to compensate. Build up the revs as you complete the turn.

▲ **Warn your crew before you start high-speed manoeuvres.**

High-speed turns are fun in good conditions, but if the waves are too large, or if you have any doubts about your ability or the seaworthiness of your boat, then avoid them. If you make a mistake you could flip your boat, and that is no fun at all.

▼ **Throttle back a little for a tight turn**

## ENGINE TRIM

The angle of an outboard or outdrive can be altered to vary the thrust direction of the propeller. Basically, with the engine angled down the propeller pushes downwards, raising the stern and lowering the bow. Lifting the engine angles the propeller up, so it tends to push the stern down and raise the bow.

At first it is a good idea to set the trim level, but as you gain experience you will find that varying the trim can improve performance, particularly when you are up on the plane or executing tight turns under power.

Trimming the engine up during a straight-line run reduces friction between the hull and the water, enabling the boat to travel smoothly, quickly and economically. It will also reduce wear and tear on the engine itself. Trimming the engine down when cornering lowers the forward hull sections to give better 'grip' on the water.

### On the plane
Trim down as you pull away to keep the hull level in the water, and apply the power progressively to lift the boat up onto the plane. Once you are planing trim the engine up to lift the bow until the boat starts to porpoise, then trim down just a touch. With the bow out of the water, the bow wave moves astern, your speed increases and the engine runs smoother.

### Tight turns under power
Approach the turn with the engine trimmed slightly up as above, then trim down. The bow will dip, allowing the V-hull to bite into the water. This stops the boat slipping sideways, and you will corner as if on tramlines. As you power out of the turn raise the trim to the straight-run position as before.

▶ When the engine is vertical it drives the boat level (1). Angling the propeller down tends to power the boat in a convex arc, driving the bow down (2). Angling the propeller up has the opposite effect, raising the bow (3). At the ideal angle the boat is powered clear of the water but planes cleanly across it (4).

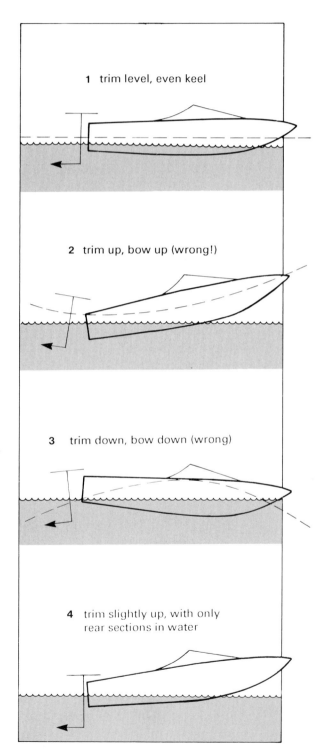

1　trim level, even keel

2　trim up, bow up (wrong!)

3　trim down, bow down (wrong)

4　trim slightly up, with only rear sections in water

Trimming up pushes the bow out of the water, but it also makes the stern dig in, creating drag.

Trimming down pushes the bow down, increasing friction but improving directional stability.

If you get it right the boat will fly across the water, and use less fuel in the process.

## WAVE JUMPING

When the waves are not too steep and not too far apart, a small high-speed planing craft can handle them at top speed, literally skimming over the top. If the tide is travelling with the wind you will have a fairly easy ride, but if it is against the wind the waves will be blown into steep, sharp peaks and the ride will be hard and lumpy. You may have to slow down.

Negotiating big waves requires a different technique. Instead of skimming across the crests the boat will ride up and over each wave individually. If you get it wrong you may flip the boat over, or plunge through the wave instead of over it.

The boat will often ride over the crest fairly well and then hurtle down the back of the wave, aiming at the steep face of the next wave. You must keep the bow up to avoid the submarine effect, so move the crew towards the stern, trim the engine up to lift the bow or use the trim tabs, if fitted.

Never reduce power as you meet a large wave as this will cause the bow to drop and you may bury it into the wall of water. But as you ride up and over the wave, throttle back – otherwise you will carry on up towards the sky, and may even flip over backwards. Even if you avoid this you

will be airborne with the wave trough several metres below you, and as you fall out of the sky you may plunge straight into the bottom of the next approaching wave.

Once you are over the crest, power on to ride up the next wave and reduce power as you near the crest. Once again, aim to stay in contact with the water as you peak the wave and then power on down the back.

## HEAVY WEATHER

If you set off from a marina or sheltered harbour and meet really rough water, slow down immediately but maintain a steady speed to prevent waves breaking over and inboard.

If you want to change direction, wait until you encounter a relatively flat piece of water between the waves. It may take time to find this, but it will be there. Turn quickly and apply enough power to avoid being caught up in the waves. You will need a lot of power to climb up to the crest of the next approaching wave, and it is often wise to ride on the back of a wave or close to the top until you reach quieter water.

The most important advice concerning heavy weather is to avoid it if you can. Never go looking for bad weather: it will find you soon enough.

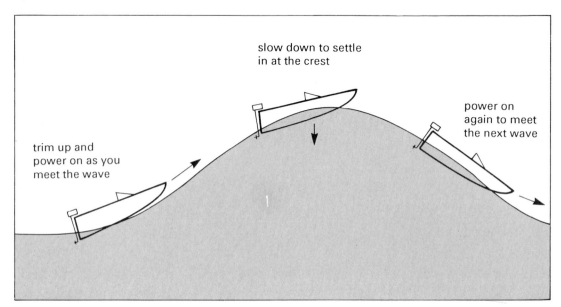

slow down to settle
in at the crest

power on
again to meet
the next wave

trim up and
power on as you
meet the wave

# 6 Rules of the road

Whether you are planing across the wavetops or just gurgling along, you are not alone. Other craft are out there too: sailing dinghies, fishing boats, yachts, tramp steamers, ocean liners, hovercraft, even submarines. Sooner or later you will find yourself in confrontation with one of these vessels. You will need to know what to do.

The rules of the road – otherwise known as the International Regulations for Preventing Collisions at Sea – are designed to cover every type of confrontation between sea-going vessels, regardless of size, speed and purpose. You need to be aware of them, so that you understand your rights and obligations on the water. It is not simply a matter of power giving way to sail. For example, a deep-drafted cargo vessel in a narrow channel has no obligation to give way to a small yacht.

It is important to realize that the rules are intended to cover close encounters between vessels. In congested waters such close encounters are inevitable, but on the open sea you can avoid them. If you keep well clear of other craft, the question of who gives way will not arise. This is good seamanship. But if you get so close that there is a real risk of collision, you must know what to do. It's no good diving into the bag for the rule book when you are hurtling towards another powerboat at a closing speed of 40 knots. You have to KNOW.

Some of the most important rules are given here in readily-understood form. Try to learn them by heart. Then go out and buy yourself a copy of *A Small Boat Guide to the Rules of the Road*, also published by Fernhurst Books. It will keep you out of trouble, wherever you go on the water.

## Rule 5: Lookout
Maintain a proper lookout at all times. Use sight and hearing.

## Rule 6: Safe Speed
Moderate your speed to ensure that you have the stopping distance to avoid a collision. Take account of the visibility, state of the waves, weather, traffic density, depth of water and manoeuvrability.

## Rule 7: Risk of collision
Correct anti-collision procedure must be followed at all times. Even if there seems to be only slight risk of collision, assume the worst and avoid the situation.

Take bearings on vessels approaching or crossing. If the visual or compass bearing does not change appreciably, then a collision could be imminent.

**◄ If the bearing of an approaching boat stays constant you are heading for collision.**

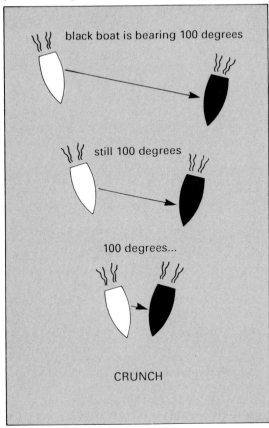

black boat is bearing 100 degrees

still 100 degrees

100 degrees...

CRUNCH

## Rule 8: Action to avoid collision

Make all alterations of course and speed in good time. Over-emphasise any alteration of course to indicate to the other vessel your intentions.

Do not alter course into the path of other vessels.

Do not stand on your rights. The other vessel may not be aware of the collision regulations. Stop and consider going into reverse.

## Rule 9: Narrow channels

Keep to the starboard side of the channel, and pass oncoming craft port to port. Do not impede larger vessels. Ensure there is sufficient water when overtaking. Maintain a sensible speed at all times.

## Rule 10: Traffic separation schemes

Small craft should, if possible, avoid Traffic Separation Schemes. If using the lanes, try to join at their beginning or end. If joining elsewhere, filter in at a very small angle, rather as you would join a motorway from a slip road. When crossing the lanes, cross at as near 90° as possible. Do not cross directly in front of vessels using the lanes.

## Rule 13: Overtaking

The overtaking vessel shall keep clear (while the vessel being overtaken shall maintain its course).

A vessel is overtaking when it approaches from astern of the other craft, anywhere in the area covered by the white stern light. If you are overhauling another vessel and you are in any doubt of the angle, then you should consider yourself to be overtaking.

## Rule 14: Head-on situation

Two power-driven vessels approaching each other shall each alter course to starboard and shall pass port to port. If in any doubt, always alter course to starboard, *never* to port.

However, if there is no danger of a collision, do not alter course merely to pass port to port. In practice, many vessels pass each other at a distance starboard to starboard. The rule is intended to remove confusion in the event of a potential collision, not as a rigid scheme of lane discipline.

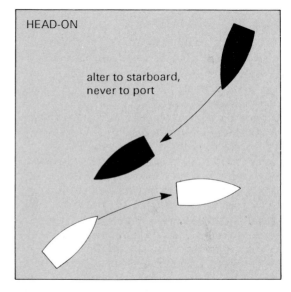

HEAD-ON

alter to starboard, never to port

◄ Always alter to starboard if you are approaching head-on, or nearly head-on. The other boat should do the same (as below) and all will be well.

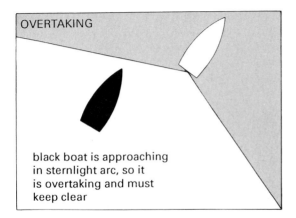

OVERTAKING

black boat is approaching in sternlight arc, so it is overtaking and must keep clear

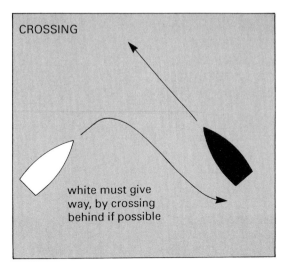

CROSSING

white must give way, by crossing behind if possible

➤ **If a crossing vessel is approaching on your starboard bow you must give way to it.**

### Rule 15: Crossing situation
When two powerboats are crossing, the vessel which has the other on its starboard side shall keep out of its way. Try to avoid crossing ahead of the vessel that has 'right of way'.

### Rule 16: Action by give-way vessel
Every vessel taking avoiding action shall do so in plenty of time and keep well clear.

### Rule 17: Action by stand-on vessel
If you have 'right of way' you should maintain your course and speed. However, if the 'give-way' vessel fails to give way, you should take whatever action is necessary to avoid a collision. (This rule does not relieve the 'give-way' vessel of the obligation to keep out of the way.)

If a crossing vessel fails to respond and give way, the 'stand-on' vessel should never alter course to port for a vessel on its port side. If in doubt, always alter to starboard.

### Rule 18: Responsibility between vessels
Power-driven vessels underway shall keep out of the way of the following:
● a vessel not under command.
● a vessel restricted in its ability to manoeuvre.
● a vessel engaged in fishing.
● a vessel under sail.

Note that a sailing vessel being propelled by its sails *and* engine is considered a power-driven vessel, and should indicate that it is under power by exhibiting a conical shape, apex downwards, somewhere forward in the rigging.

### Rule 34: Manoeuvring and warning signals
Power-driven vessels underway may indicate their intentions by the following sound signals:
● One short blast = I am altering my course to starboard
●● Two short blasts = I am altering my course to port
●●● Three short blasts = I am operating astern propulsion (but could still be moving ahead).
These signals are usually given with the horn, but a flashing light can be used instead.

## LIGHTS AND SHAPES

### Rule 23: Power-driven vessels underway
Vessels less than 50 metres in length should display:
1 A white light at the masthead.
2 A red port light and green starboard light (see diagram).
3 A white stern light.
Vessels less than 12 metres in length need only display:
1 An all-round white light.
2 Red port and green starboard sidelights.
Vessels less than seven metres in length, travelling at less than seven knots, need only display:
1 An all-round white light.
Larger vessels, and vessels engaged in special activities, all have prescribed lights to be displayed at night and shapes to be displayed by day. You should become familiar with these, since such vessels may have right-of-way over you, or may constitute a hazard.

### Rule 35: Sound signals in restricted visibility
Restricted visibility means fog, falling snow or heavy rain. In such conditions a power-driven vessel underway shall make one prolonged blast on the horn at intervals of not more than two minutes.

# 7 Mooring

However much you enjoy using your powerboat, at some point you will want to stop. This is no simple matter, for if you just turn off the engine you will drift with the wind and current. You need to secure the boat, either by anchoring or – more easily – by picking up a mooring buoy.

You should aim to approach the mooring in a controlled manner and pick it up easily without using reverse gear. To do this, you have to be aware of:

- wind direction and strength.
- current direction and strength.
- wind and current direction combined.

You also need to consider:

- weight of boat
- speed of boat
- available room to manoeuvre

To determine the wind direction, look at rising smoke, flags and the direction of the waves and ripples. Waves are created by the wind and, if they are undisturbed by other craft, they will always be at 90° to the wind.

To find the direction of the current, look at the mooring buoy itself. Which way is it leaning? Watch the swirl of water around posts and jetties: the wave pattern round the obstacle will show you the water direction.

In practice, the combined effect of wind and current will be indicated by the position of other craft on their moorings – but remember that a shallow-drafted sportsboat will be less influenced by the current than a deep-keeled yacht, and more affected by the wind. Also, not all boats are on swinging moorings. Some boats are fixed to moorings at both bow and stern and should be disregarded as indicators of wind or water direction. Always plan an escape route in case you have misjudged the conditions.

**◄ Here the direction of the current is indicated by the trailing pick-up buoy, and the way the mooring buoy is leaning. Note also that the moored keelboats are pointing into the current, while the shallow-drafted motorboat is being blown off by the wind. In this case the light wind favoured an approach directly into the current.**

◆ **Approach the buoy slowly, into the current/wind.**

◆ **Pick up the buoy on the starboard side.**

1 Slowly approach the mooring buoy from the direction of downtide-downwind, in a straight line. Gradually reduce speed until there is only a short distance between the boat and mooring.

2 Put the engine into neutral and let the weight of the boat carry you forward. If your judgement is accurate, you will stop with the buoy either on the bow or alongside. With most sportsboats it is easier to pick it up from alongside. If you are travelling through the water too fast, you could ride straight over the top of it. Engaging reverse gear could help to stop you in time, but it's messy. Practise until you are able to stop by the buoy without using reverse.

3 Pick up the mooring buoy and, using the painter (rope attached to the bow), secure the boat to the chain or steel ring with a round turn and two half hitches.

4 Once secure, drop the mooring and painter over the side. The boat will drift back a few metres and rest in the water in the same position as the surrounding moored boats.

Please remember that if the mooring is not owned by you it probably belongs to someone else who might return and want to use it. Visitors' moorings are often available for short-stay and overnight stops. Speak with the Harbour Master – if he doesn't speak with you first!

◆ **To leave a mooring, first warm up the engine and check carefully all around.**

◆ **Motor slowly forward until the buoy is alongside, pick up the painter and untie it from the mooring chain.**

◀ **Secure the painter to the mooring chain.**

◀ **Drift back to take up the slack and stop the engine.**

## Leaving moorings

1 Start the engine and allow it a short warm-up period. Check around you to ensure that there are no other craft hindering your departure.
2 Engage forward gear on tick-over and use just enough power to bring you alongside the mooring. When alongside, use your hand or a boathook to pick up your painter and cast off from the mooring buoy. Secure the painter.
3 Allow the wind or tide to drift you off the mooring and, when you are clear, move slowly ahead. As you turn, remember that the directional thrust of the propeller will kick the stern out: be careful not to propel the stern in the direction of the mooring and ride over it.

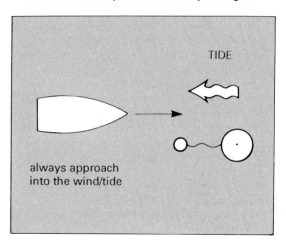

TIDE

always approach
into the wind/tide

▶ **Secure the painter in the boat and allow the wind or tide to drift the boat away from the mooring.**

▶ **Once you are well clear, engage forward gear and motor off, avoiding the buoys and any lines in the water.**

◀ **If the wind or tide is pushing you away from the jetty, approach slowly at a shallow angle.**

◀ **As you get near, go into neutral and spin the wheel towards the jetty.**

### Coming alongside a moored boat

Once you have mastered picking up a mooring buoy, coming alongside a moored boat is easy. Just follow the same method. Select your side of approach and prepare the painter and fenders (inflatable boats do not need fenders). You are now ready to make a slow, controlled approach. If you are tying onto the boat, pass your painter through a fairlead (if fitted) and tie it to a strong point such as a cleat.

### Coming alongside a jetty or pontoon

The procedure for coming alongside a jetty is much the same, but you have to take account of

the fact that a jetty or pontoon is a more or less immovable object, being attached to the land.

1 Establish a direction of approach, in a straight line if possible, against the wind and/or tide. Put out fenders (if necessary) and prepare your bow and stern lines.

2 Slowly move forward towards the jetty. Judge your speed, put the boat into neutral and let the wind or tide act as a brake to your forward motion.

3 You should slide to a halt alongside. Taking the prepared bow and stern lines, step ashore and secure them to a cleat, using a figure-of-eight lashing, or a bollard, using a bowline knot.

◀ **To leave, untie all but one of the mooring lines. Make sure you can slip the remaining line from the boat.**

◀ **Climb aboard and start up. Ensure the engine is warmed up before you cast off.**

◆ Engage reverse gear to slow the boat down and pull the stern into the jetty.

◆ Come into neutral as the boat drifts alonside, and quickly secure the boat with a mooring rope.

If wind and/or tides prevent a straight-line approach, you will have to come in at an angle. This can be tricky if the wind is strong enough to blow the bows off.

1 Approach slowly. When you get close to the jetty come into neutral.
2 Allow the weight of the boat to carry you forward, spin the steering wheel quickly towards the jetty and engage reverse gear. This will arrest your forward movement and, at the same time, pull the stern into the jetty.
3 As soon as the boat has stopped moving forward, come into neutral. Step ashore and secure the craft.

### Leaving the jetty

1 Warm up the engine and check the tide to decide which mooring lines can be taken off and stowed, leaving one attached to hold you safely against the jetty.
2 If you are leaving forwards, you will have to push the bow away from the jetty. This prevents the stern being trapped against the jetty. Alternatively, it may be preferable to leave astern because it is the stern which pulls away from the jetty when the engine is in reverse. Wind and water movement will also influence the direction of departure.
3 Having decided, cast off and move away.

◆ Slip the final mooring line and push the bow away from the jetty. Make sure the steering is centralised.

◆ Motor away in a straight line to prevent the stern veering over towards the jetty.

# ANCHORING

If you need to stop and there is no convenient mooring to tie your boat to, you will have to drop the anchor. You need to be prepared for this, with a good anchor, sufficient chain and warp, and a knowledge of the area where you intend anchoring.

## Types of anchor

**CQR (Plough)** A good-quality anchor which holds very well, but can be awkward to stow.
**Danforth** A flat anchor which stows easily and holds well.
**Grapnel** This has four flukes, only two of which enter the ground. If it is used in a sportsboat, a very much heavier anchor and chain will be required to do the same work as the other anchors listed. The grapnel is often carried in dinghies as it folds up and stows easily.
**Fisherman's** The traditional anchor, this holds well on rocky bottoms and most other types of ground.
**Bruce** A relatively new anchor, this has excellent holding properties in mud, sand and shingle. It does not require the same weight as some of the others, and is recommended for sportsboats.

All anchors are only as good as the tackle attached to them. The anchor has to be shackled to at least two metres of good-quality chain, and the chain is attached to a warp (anchor rope) which should be at least 30 metres long. Avoid using buoyant polypropylene rope for the warp, for this will entangle passing boats. Use nylon or polyester, which sink and have the elasticity to absorb shock as the boat is washed to and fro in the waves.

## Stowage

Big boats usually have special stowage compartments for anchors (chain or anchor lockers) but this is unusual on a small sportsboat. Yet even without an anchor locker, it is an easy job to store the anchor, chain and rope.

Obtain a large plastic crate. This will prevent the anchor and rope from spreading around the boat and becoming entangled. Flake the rope down into the crate, so it is ready for use without any kinks or knots in it. Cut a small hole in the side of the crate, pass the end of the rope through it

⬆ A plough anchor (left) and a Danforth anchor (right).

and secure it to the boat. Lay the chain on top of the rope and finally place the anchor in.

Stretch an elastic cord over the top of the crate to keep everything in place. You should also secure the crate to the boat to stop it sliding around in heavy seas.

⬇ A chain locker is well worth having. This one contains a Bruce anchor, chain and polyester warp.

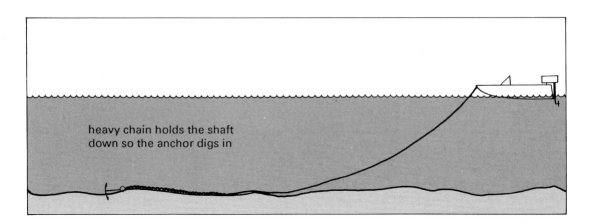

heavy chain holds the shaft
down so the anchor digs in

It is worthwhile spending money and time ensuring that this vital equipment is on board and in working order. It may·seem an unnecessary expense but, in reality, it is part of your insurance premium – it could save not only your boat, but also your life.

### Preparing the tackle

Mark your rope at two-metre intervals with bands of coloured twine. You can read off the bands as you pay out the rope, so when the weight of the anchor and chain reach the bottom and go slack, you know the approximate depth. You should then multiply this depth of water by five, to give the approximate amount of rope to be lowered over the side.

You need this length of rope because the anchor will only dig in if the weight of the chain pulls horizontally along the sea, lake or river bed. The chain will only pull horizontally if the rope attached to it also pulls horizontally along the ground – and it will only do this if you lower enough rope.

### Holding ground

Check that the sea (lake or river) bed is good holding ground. Ask someone who has local knowledge, and check on the chart for designated anchorages and areas where anchoring is prohibited. Among the obvious prohibited areas are those where electric power lines run, deep-water navigation channels, warship exercise areas, among moorings and between ferry terminals. Do not anchor close to other vessels: remember that they, and you, will

◄ **A long anchor warp gives the right angle of pull.**

swing with the wind and tide, and you may collide.

Few sportsboats have depth sounders, so you will have to check the chart and tide table to find the depth of water under your keel (see Chapter 9).

◄ **Check the chart to make sure anchoring is permitted. The chart may also show recommended anchorages.**

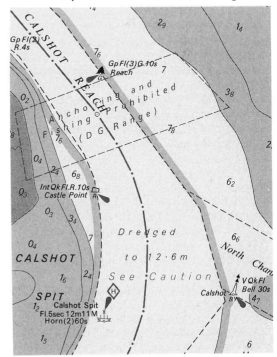

⬆ **When you are in position, lower the anchor over the side.**

⬆ **When it touches, measure off the rope and multiply by five.**

⬆ **Pay out the rope you need as you drift back in the tide.**

## Anchoring technique

1 Check the area to decide which is the stronger force, tide or wind. If you are unsure, come into neutral and check your drift against stationary objects such as other craft at anchor, trees on the shore and buildings.

2 Engage forward gear and slowly drive to a position ahead of where you wish to stop, pointing into the wind and/or tide. As you start to drift backwards, instruct the crew to lower the anchor over the side.

3 When the anchor touches the bottom the weight goes off the warp. Read off the bands on the warp, multiply by five and slowly lower this length of warp as the boat drifts backwards and sideways. Do not expect the anchor to hold until the line is out to the required depth.

4 When you are satisfied that sufficient line is out, tie it off and allow the boat to pull on the warp. Engage reverse and go backwards slowly to dig the anchor in. The boat will lurch gently to a stop once the anchor gains a hold.

5 If it does not hold, the boat will keep drifting, and you have two choices: go into neutral and let out more warp or raise the anchor and try again.

6 As soon as it holds firmly, go into neutral. The warp will now be fairly tight over the side and the boat will rest at about 45° to the wind and/or tide. Take the painter (bow rope) and, using a double sheet bend onto the anchor warp, transfer the weight of the anchor to the painter. The bow will now face the wind and/or tide.

## Tidal waters

At sea, or in a tidal river, you will need to lay out more cable to allow for rising tide. As the tide falls the boat will drift back further and swing round in the tidal stream. Make sure you have room.

## Transits

When you are satisfied that the anchor is holding, check for any fixed objects in the vicinity that line up to form transits. Two such transit alignments define your position. Re-check from time to time to make sure the anchor is not dragging – but remember to allow for tidal effects. If you cannot see any good alignments, take compass bearings on isolated objects such as buoys and towers, and re-check these at intervals (see Chapter 9).

⬅ **Two transit alignments will provide a ready check on your anchored position.**

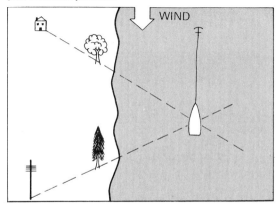

⬆ **When you have laid enough, tie the boat's painter to the anchor rope.**

⬆ **Allow the boat to drift back. The pull on the painter will drag the bow into the wind and/or tide.**

### Raising the anchor

1 Start up the engine and warm up.
2 With a fairly light sportsboat, the crew can slowly pull in the warp and the boat will creep forward through the water without using the engine. A heavy craft will probably need a push with the engine but be careful not to overrun the anchor warp.
3 The crew should release the painter from the anchor warp and make the painter secure in the boat. As he retrieves the anchor warp, he can flake down the rope into the anchor box so it is ready for the next time.
4 When the boat is directly over the anchor the warp will be vertical, and a good heave should break the anchor out of the sea bed.

5 The boat is now drifting, but do not engage gear until the anchor is clear of the water. Keep the anchor and chain clear from the side of the boat to prevent damage. Remove any mud and place the chain and then the anchor on top of the warp in the box. Check the direction of drift, decide whether to move ahead or astern, then slowly drive away.

### Tripping lines

What should you do if the anchor refuses to come up? The conventional type of tripping line creates too much confusion of rope for a small powerboat, but you can rig an automatic tripping device; if you are anchoring on an unknown sea bed, it might be useful.

⬇ **To raise the anchor, haul forward and untie the painter.**

⬇ **Haul in the rope. You may need help from the engine.**

⬇ **A vertical pull will free the anchor, and you can haul it in.**

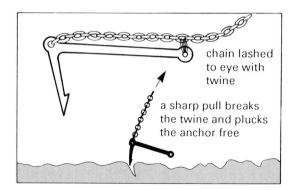

Set the anchor up with the chain attached at the hook end. Lash the eye in the shaft to the chain with thin twine, as shown in the diagram. If the anchor fails to lift, a sharp tug on the warp will break the twine and the anchor should lift from the shackled end.

Continually check the condition of the twine, otherwise the anchor could trip out of the sea bed under normal use. The twine will perish and will need replacing regularly. Note that this method is not suitable for heavy boat, which will simply snap the twine as soon as the anchor bites in the sea bed.

## ROPEWORK

Competence in handling ropes and knots should be second nature to boat handlers. You need ropes for mooring, anchoring and towing, as well as rescue. Ropework is no mystery: it only takes practice. Remember that a little dexterity with ropes could save your life.

Always use good quality ropes of the right material. The rope must be strong enough for the job required of it but, at the same time, it must fit comfortably in the hand and be pleasant to handle.

### Care of rope
Wash rope thoroughly with fresh water. Remove sand, grit and mud, and hang it up to dry. Do not leave wet rope in the bottom of the boat.

Avoid the pretty coil. This is difficult to use when it dries out. It is better to loop the rope along the side of the boat if you do not have the facilities to hang it up.

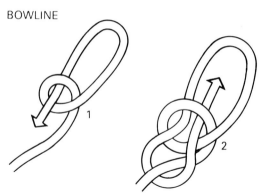

### Bowline
This is probably the most useful knot of them all. It can be used for mooring, joining two ropes together, towing the boat and trailer out of the water and looping around the chest of a person in the water. It cannot collapse or slip and it can always be quickly undone once the load is off, regardless of how much weight has been put on it.

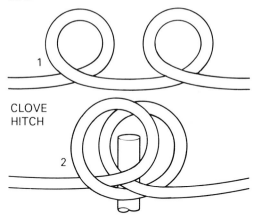

### Clove hitch
This is useful for forming a strong hitch in the middle of a rope which is attached at both ends. It is the one you use on the towing ball of the vehicle for retrieving the boat and trailer. No matter how heavy a load it has to bear, it can easily be worked loose afterwards.

Take the rope and form two loops, both in the same direction. Place the top loop behind the other loop and drop both over the ball hitch or bollard. The load can be applied from both directions at the same time, or from one direction only.

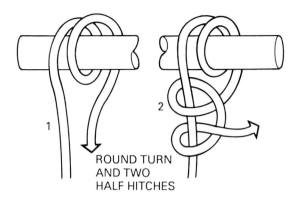

ROUND TURN
AND TWO
HALF HITCHES

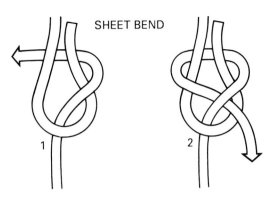

SHEET BEND

### Round turn and two half hitches

This is another very useful hitch, excellent for tying up to mooring buoys.

For the round turn, put two loops around the ring. Then finish off with two half hitches. They should look like a clove hitch secured around the standing part of the rope.

### Sheet bend

This is used for joining two ropes together and is especially valuable if they are of different thicknesses. Both loose ends can be seized (whipped with twine) to the standing parts to make a more permanent bend.

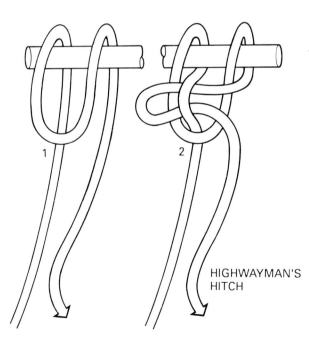

HIGHWAYMAN'S
HITCH

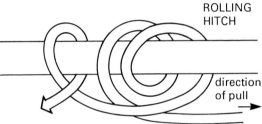

ROLLING
HITCH

direction
of pull

### Rolling hitch

This is excellent for a side pull on another rope or wire, but make sure the pull is from the direction shown.

CAMEL HITCH

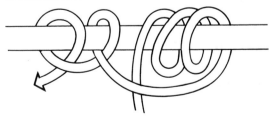

### Highwayman's hitch

This slip knot is recommended when you need to leave a jetty or mooring fairly rapidly especially if the boat is tied to a high post out of reach of the boat. When you are ready to go, pull the free end and the hitch will collapse.

### Camel hitch

The camel hitch will take strain from both directions and can easily be undone even if soaking wet. It is excellent for towing a line of dinghies astern on one tow line.

# 8 Tidal waters

Tides are caused by water being dragged across the Earth's surface by the gravitational pull of the moon and sun.

The moon has the greatest effect: as it orbits the Earth it tends to pull the water with it. In many parts of the world the tide is also high when the moon is on the opposite side of the Earth. The two high tides occur roughly 12 hours apart, separated by low tides.

The sun's effect is much less obvious, but still important. Basically, its gravitational pull either reinforces that of the moon, or acts against it. When the sun and moon are in line they work together: the tide is pulled up extra-high and falls extra-low. The cycle of high to low water is called a spring tide. When the sun and moon are at right angles they act against each other, and the tide rise and fall is relatively slight. This is called a neap tide.

The position of the sun relative to the moon is obvious to us because of the way the moon is illuminated. When the sun and moon are at right angles the moon is lit from the side and appears as a half-moon. When the sun and moon are in line the moon is lit either from the front, giving a full moon, or from the back, giving a dark or new moon. So at half moon we experience a neap tide, and at full or new moon we get a spring.

## PREDICTING THE TIDE

The phases of the moon work on a 28-day cycle and so do the tides, as follows:

● Day 1 – new moon – spring tide
◐ Day 7 – half moon – neap tide
○ Day 14 – full moon – spring tide
◑ Day 21 – half moon – neap tide
● Day 28 – new moon again

On each intervening day the tide is intermediate between a neap and a spring, grading smoothly from one to the other.

↞ During a neap tide (top) the water level does not rise or fall very far. A spring tide (bottom) rises and falls much further, and the current created by the tidal stream usually flows much faster.

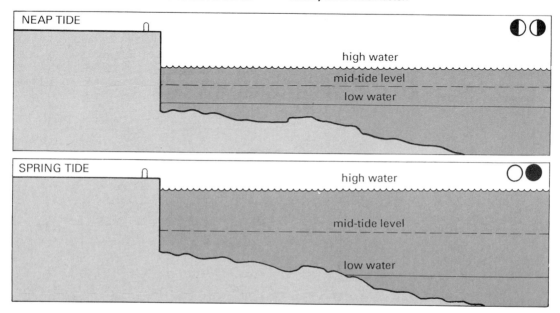

NEAP TIDE

high water
mid-tide level
low water

SPRING TIDE

high water
mid-tide level
low water

From this it might seem that you could predict the tides with some confidence, with a spring tide every other Tuesday, say. But it is not so easy. For one thing, the moon orbits the Earth not once a day, but once every 24 hours and 50 minutes (on average). This means that High Water is roughly 50 minutes later each day. What's more, there is a two-day time lag between the moon phase and the corresponding tidal effect.

Add to this the influence of local geography, which creates different heights of tide at different points on the coast, plus the fact that the moon is constantly changing its orbiting speed and distance, and it becomes obvious that predicting the tide is no simple matter.

The answer is to buy a tide table, where it is all worked out for you. The table contains the time and height of high and low water for every day in the current year. Last year's table is no good, since all the figures change.

Although the tidal heights vary all along the coast, compiling a tide table for every stretch of water would be impracticable. Instead, you obtain a table for your nearest *Standard Port*. This has the same basic tidal characteristics as your area, but there is usually a time difference and a height difference. This is indicated in the table, and you must either add or subtract the difference every time you use it.

➤ **The tide table gives the time and height of high and low water at a particular port for every day in the year — but the figures must be related to those on the chart.**

## Using the tide table

Let us assume that you want to find the time of High Water in the afternoon of 16 March.

1 Check the local time. Is your watch set to the time system indicated in the table? (In Britain, for example, this would be Greenwich Mean Time, or GMT.) Or is it set to some other time system? For this example you have to add an hour for local summer time; the table will tell you.

2 Check the tidal difference from the Standard Port. For this example you have to subtract 25 minutes from the time indicated for High Water, and deduct 0.4 metres from the height. This information will be given on the table.

3 Turn to the month in question and find the right day:

| 16 March | Time | Metres | |
|---|---|---|---|
| | 0440 | 6.5 | (HW) |
| | 1041 | 0.5 | (LW) |
| | 1640 | 6.9 | (HW) |
| | 2315 | 0.8 | (LW) |

4 Add 35 minutes to the time given, subtract 0.4 metres from the height, and you have the answer:

1715   6.5 metres

Remember that the tidal height is the height of water to be added to the height given on the chart (see Chapter 9). This means that you will almost certainly have less water, or more. If you are aiming to launch a boat from a slip that dries out at Low Water, you will have to check this.

---

# IRELAND, WEST COAST - GALWAY

### LAT 53°16′N   LONG 9°03′W

TIME ZONE **GMT**   TIMES AND HEIGHTS OF HIGH AND LOW WATERS   YEAR **1986**

| | SEPTEMBER | | | | OCTOBER | | | | NOVEMBER | | | | DECEMBER | | |
|---|---|---|---|---|---|---|---|---|---|---|---|---|---|---|---|
| | TIME | M | | TIME | M | | TIME | M | | TIME | M | | TIME | M | TIME | M |
| **1** 0331 4.0 / 0925 1.7 / M 1542 4.2 / 2157 1.3 | **16** 0339 4.6 / 0934 1.1 / TU 1545 4.9 / 2159 0.6 | **1** 0338 4.4 / 0929 1.4 / W 1543 4.6 / 2155 0.9 | **16** 0356 4.9 / 0949 1.0 / TH 1603 5.1 / 2209 0.7 | **1** 0404 5.1 / 0959 0.8 / SA 1614 5.2 / 2220 0.6 | **16** 0438 5.0 / 1037 1.1 / SU 1652 4.9 / O 2248 1.1 | **1** 0410 5.3 / 1013 0.8 / M 1631 5.3 / ● 2234 0.8 | **16** 0452 4.9 / 1101 1.3 / TU 1715 4.6 / O 2305 1.5 |
| **2** 0409 4.2 / 1000 1.4 / TU 1616 4.4 / 2230 1.0 | **17** 0420 4.8 / 1013 0.8 / W 1627 5.2 / 2235 0.4 | **2** 0409 4.7 / 1000 1.1 / TH 1614 4.9 / 2224 0.6 | **17** 0431 5.0 / 1024 0.8 / F 1640 5.2 / O 2242 0.6 | **2** 0440 5.3 / 1035 0.6 / SU 1654 5.3 / ● 2257 0.5 | **17** 0512 5.1 / 1113 1.1 / M 1730 4.9 / 2322 1.2 | **2** 0454 5.5 / 1057 0.6 / TU 1718 5.3 / 2318 0.8 | **17** 0529 4.9 / 1139 1.3 / W 1754 4.6 / 2342 1.5 |
| **3** 0441 4.5 / 1033 1.1 / W 1648 4.7 / 2259 0.7 | **18** 0457 5.0 / 1049 0.6 / TH 1705 5.3 / O 2311 0.3 | **3** 0440 4.9 / 1031 0.8 / F 1647 5.1 / ● 2254 0.4 | **18** 0505 5.1 / 1059 0.7 / SA 1716 5.2 / 2315 0.7 | **3** 0516 5.4 / 1113 0.5 / M 1734 5.4 / 2334 0.6 | **18** 0546 5.0 / 1149 1.2 / TU 1807 4.8 / 2356 1.4 | **3** 0537 5.5 / 1143 0.6 / W 1807 5.3 | **18** 0604 4.8 / 1217 1.3 / TH 1832 4.6 |
| **4** 0513 4.7 / 1102 … | … 0533 5.1 | **4** 0512 5.1 / … | **19** 0539 5… | … 0556 5.5 | **19** 0621 4.9 / … | … 0003 1.0 / 0641 4.8 | **19** 0018 1.6 / … |

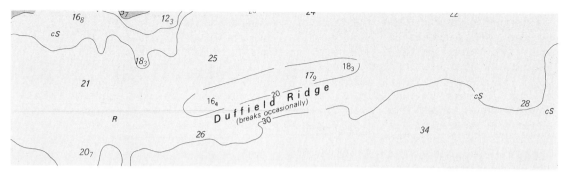

If you need to know the approximate depth of water at 0840 hours, you can use the Twelfths Rule, a rough and ready rule of thumb. First find the range by subtracting the Low Water height from the High Water height:

|     |             |
| --- | ----------- |
| HW  | 6.5 metres  |
| LW  | 0.5 metres  |
|     |             |
| Range | 6.0 metres |

Then divide the range by 12:

$$6.0 \div 12 = 0.5 \text{ metres}$$

The rate at which the tide falls (and rises) can be expressed in terms of this figure:

In the first hour it falls $\frac{1}{12} = 0.5$ metres
In the second hour it falls $\frac{2}{12} = 1.0$ metres
In the third hour it falls $\frac{3}{12} = 1.5$ metres
In the fourth hour it falls $\frac{3}{12} = 1.5$ metres
In the fifth hour it falls $\frac{2}{12} = 1.0$ metres
In the sixth hour it falls $\frac{1}{12} = 0.5$ metres

You wanted to know the depth of water at 0840. This is four hours after High Water, so add the hours up like this:

| First hour:   | 0.5 metres |
| ------------- | ---------- |
| Second hour:  | 1.0 metres |
| Third hour:   | 1.5 metres |
| Fourth hour   | 1.5 metres |
|               |            |
|               | 4.5 metres |

You can then deduct this figure from the height of High Water: 6.5 metres − 4.5 metres = 2.0 metres *above the figure on the chart.* Note that the figures used here are the figures for the Standard Port. If you are operating some way down the coast you will need to modify these before you start the calculation (and correct them for local time).

◆ **The chart shows the depth of water at the lowest possible tide. Any tidal height given in the tide table (or one you work out yourself) has to be added to the figures on the chart to give the true depth of water.**

Look at it from another angle: at High Water the tide has reached its maximum height and holds this for a short while before starting to fall. In the first hour it falls slowly, then speeds up during the second hour. It falls fastest during the third and fourth hours, before slowing down to stop at Low Water. It follows the same pattern as it rises.

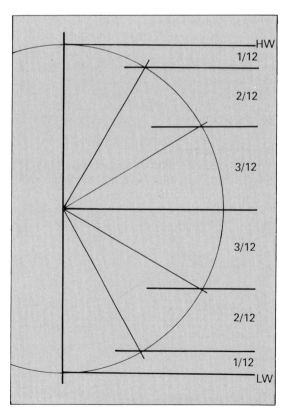

Naturally the actual rate of fall will depend on how far it is going to drop: during a spring tide it will fall much faster than during a neap.

## TIDAL STREAMS

As tide rises and falls, so the body of water moves back and forth. Tidal streams are the horizontal movement of water, *flooding* as the tide rises and *ebbing* as it goes out. Referring to the Twelfths Rule, it is easy to see that the movement at High Water is virtually nil. In the first hour of a tide it begins to speed up, quickening for the second hour and becoming faster still for the third and fourth, before slowing down again until it stops at Low Water. During a spring tide the flow will move that much faster than during a neap tide.

Apart from the obvious problem of fighting a strong tidal stream with inadequate power, you can also get into trouble where a large body of moving water is squeezing through a narrow channel or over a shallow area. As the speed of water increases it swirls into whirlpools and stopper waves; in some places the water appears to boil as if it were in a cauldron. Such tide rips and overfalls often occur close to headlands, estuaries and channels, and are shown on the charts. If the water is deep enough they can be negotiated at the right state of the tide (usually slack water), but they are best avoided.

### Steering in a cross-tide

When you are travelling at high speed across a tidal stream your sideways drift is minimal, but if you are motoring at slow displacement speed the current will push you off course. Simply aiming for your goal is no help: you will still drift sideways and finish up approaching from the wrong angle. The best approach is to align your goal visually with something behind it, such as a headland or tree, and keep them aligned as you travel. This 'transit' will keep you on track regardless of any tidal effects.

◀ **This graphic representation of the Twelfths Rule shows how the rate of tidal rise or fall speeds up and slows down.**

▶ **A boat that is steered using a transit will stay on track in a cross-tide, but a boat that is simply aimed at its goal may drift sideways into danger.**

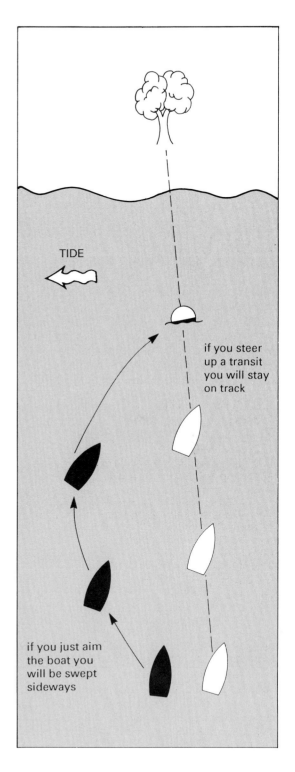

TIDE

if you steer up a transit you will stay on track

if you just aim the boat you will be swept sideways

# 9 Charts, buoys and pilotage

Like most powerboat users you will probably spend a lot of time in home waters that you know fairly well, but eventually you may want to venture further afield. You will need to know where you can go and where you can't, and you will also need some means of judging your position out there on the open water. For this you must know something about charts, buoys and pilotage.

## CHARTS

It is very difficult to handle a chart in a small boat. Very few sportsboats have any space where you can lay out a chart without it blowing away or getting soaked. Yet it is always wise to keep an up-to-date chart of the area somewhere on the boat. Since conventional paper charts fall to pieces when wet, it is a good idea to buy the new all-weather waterproof charts. You can keep the chart fixed to a clipboard or, better still, covered in transparent plastic sheeting. You could keep several sheets like this, in book form.

Charts come in all scales. The really small-scale ones are intended for ocean passages; these are of no use in small powerboats. You need large-scale charts of estuaries, harbours and coasts that show the mudbanks, sandbanks, buoys, channels, jetties, marinas and a host of other features in detail.

One of the main functions of a chart is to indicate the depth of water. It does this by a system of contour lines similar to those used on land maps to indicate heights above sea level. On a chart the depths are measured from a zero point known as Chart Datum (CD). This is a theoretical lowest possible height of water, known as Lowest Astronomical Tide (LAT). The depths may be measured in metres or fathoms; the units used are indicated at the top and bottom of the chart.

➤ **This section of chart shows a shallow channel winding between mudflats that dry out at Chart Datum. Note the underlined figures which indicate drying heights. The diagram at the top of the opposite page shows a section from A to B on the chart, with the Chart Datum marked as a solid line, a realistic one-metre low tide and a four-metre high tide.**

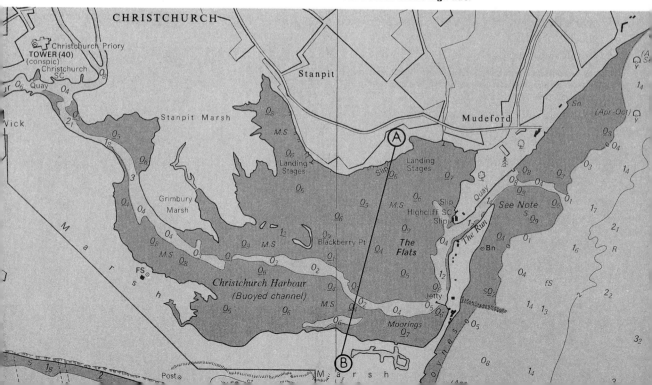

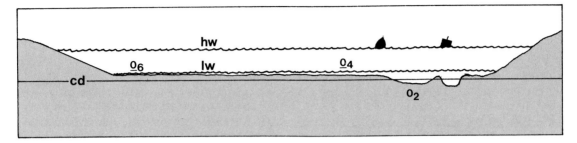

There are two types of depth figure: a 'sounding' or depth below Chart Datum, and a 'drying height' or height *above* Chart Datum. Drying heights refer to areas such as mudbanks that are often covered with water, but may dry out at low tide.

A sounding (in this case 6.5 metres) looks like this: $6_5$

Whereas a drying height (here 2.2 metres) looks like this: $\underline{2}_2$

You will recall that all tidal heights are measured from Chart Datum. To find the true depth of water at any point, you have to add the sounding to the height of tide, or subtract the drying height.

Assume that you are hoping to launch your boat into a tidal river that you have never visited. The chart indicates a sounding of 0.3 metres in the middle of the channel, and a drying height of 0.8 metres at the end of the slipway, so at first glance the launching site seems useless. So why is it there?

**The situation at the launching site in cross-section and as it appears on the chart (right). The box on the left gives the tidal information.**

A look at the tide table provides the answer. At 10.00 on the day in question, Low Water at this site is 1.4 metres, while High Water is 5.0 metres. Add the sounding to the Low Water figure, and you find there is a minimum depth of 1.7 metres in the channel. Deduct the drying height from the High Water figure, and you discover that the end of the slip is 4.2 metres beneath the surface at High Water. Since you do not want to wait around for this, you will need to find out when there will be about one metre of water at the end of the slip. Find the range, divide by 12 and work it out (see Chapter 8). Between them, the chart and the tide table have given you access to a completely new stretch of water.

## BUOYAGE

The chart will also give you details of all the buoys and beacons in the area. Many of these mark the channels needed by deep-drafted vessels, and may not concern you directly (always look at the chart to check). But they do make excellent reference points when you are out on the water, so it is worth becoming familiar with them.

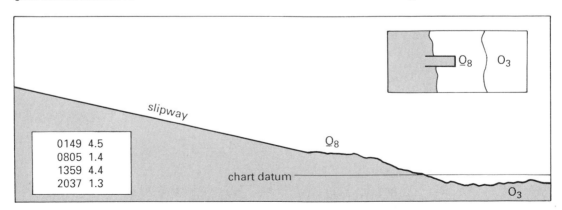

In harbours, estuaries and busy navigation routes, the deep water is marked either by posts or floating navigation marks. These are not only colour-coded and of a characteristic shape, but they are also often named or numbered. The shape, name or number also appear on the chart. Although many are floating they are precisely positioned: on the chart the little circle at the base of each symbol indicates its true position.

The colour and shape of a buoy indicates its function, but this varies according to where you are on the globe. In Europe, Africa, India, Australia and most of Asia (Region A) all the navigation marks conform to one convention, whereas in America, Japan, South Korea and the Philippines (Region B) they conform to another.

### Buoyage in Region A

There are several different types of marks. The most familiar are probably the *Lateral Marks* which indicate channels. There are two of these: starboard-hand marks (green and cone-shaped) on the right-hand side of the channel when entering a harbour or estuary from the sea, and port-hand marks (red and can-shaped) on the left-hand side. With coastal channels the lateral marks are arranged according to the tidal stream, so if you are drifting on the flood tide (the rising tide) all the greens will be on the right and all the reds on the left. Where there is no tide they are arranged in the direction of the main navigation stream.

The left and right sometimes causes confusion. A useful memory jogger is 'No red port left in the bottle'. Also, remember that port has the same number of letters in the word as left.

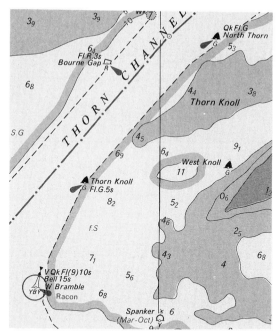

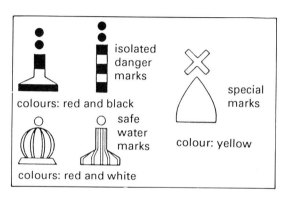

This busy channel in region 'A' is flanked by a variety of buoys, each with a name. 'Bourne Gap' is a lit port-hand red can, while 'North Thorn' and 'Thorn Knoll' are lit starboard-hand green cones. 'W Bramble' is a west Cardinal mark, indicating the western edge of a shallow area. 'Spanker' is a seasonal Special Mark used for yacht racing, while 'West Knoll' is an unlit starboard-hand mark in shallow water for small boats.

It is important to be able to recognise navigation marks by shape, because with bright sunshine behind them, or in poor visibility, their colour cannot be seen. The most important navigation marks also have flashing lights on them which are coloured and coded. These are marked on the chart in abbreviated form.

Isolated Danger, Special and Safe Water Marks.

Lateral Marks, with region 'A' and 'B' colours.

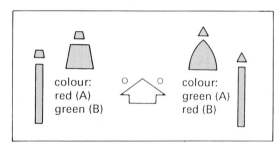

colour: red (A) green (B)

colour: green (A) red (B)

isolated danger marks — colours: red and black

safe water marks — colours: red and white

special marks — colour: yellow

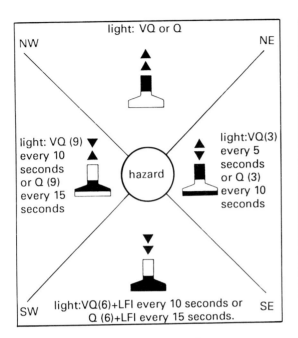

➤ **Each Cardinal Mark has its own colour pattern, topmark and light characteristics. The cones on top of a North Cardinal point up, while those on a South Cardinal point down. A West Cardinal topmark is 'wasp-waisted' while an East Cardinal topmark clearly isn't! Note that the cones on each topmark 'point' to the black bands in the colour scheme.**

Yellow marks, sometimes with a yellow cross on top, are *Special Marks*. They may be any shape that is not easily confused with other marks. They are used to indicate various things: designated waterski areas, outer perimeter marks for swimmers, lanes for jet bikes and powerboats are a few examples.

Yellow-and-black marks with two black cones on top are *Cardinal Marks*. They are placed either north, south, east or west of a hazard, and you can tell which it is by the pattern of the black cones, the arrangement of black-and-yellow stripes, and the way the light flashes.

A red-and-black mark with two black balls on top is an *Isolated Danger Mark*, placed over a wreck or an isolated rock. You can pass on either side of this, but avoid the area of the mark itself.

You may also come across a *Safe Water Mark*: a buoy with vertical red-and-white stripes. This simply acts as a signpost for large vessels.

## Buoyage in Region B

Region B covers North, South and Central America, Canada, Japan, South Korea and the Philippines. The main difference is in the Lateral Marks, for although the cone and can shapes are on the same sides as in Region A (Europe), the colours are reversed. Red is to starboard while green is to port. Otherwise the system follows the same conventions as in Region A.

Cardinal Marks, Isolated Danger Marks and Safe Water Marks are the same as in Region A. The Special Marks are also yellow, with various top marks. They are used for anchorages and moorings, and may also warn of dangers such as firing ranges, pipelines, race courses, seaplane bases and areas where no through channels exist. Some mark waters where boats are prohibited, while others are for speed control, or give information.

## PILOTAGE

Once you understand tides, charts and navigation marks you will be able to use this knowledge to fix your position in inshore waters, and work out courses to steer that avoid dangers and deliver you swiftly and safely to your destination. Most open-water navigation methods are beyond the resources of the sportsboat owner, but a few basic pilotage techniques (employed inshore where there are plenty of buoys and landmarks) are well worth mastering.

### Distance

You can measure distances on the chart using a pair of dividers transferred to the scale of latitude down both sides of the chart. The longitude scale along the top and bottom should be ignored as a means of measurement because it is distorted.

The latitude lines are parallel to the equator, with one for each degree of latitude. From the north pole to the south pole there are 180 of them, measured north and south of the equator. The 49th parallel, for example, which forms the border between the USA and Canada, is at 49° North, while Rio de Janeiro is at roughly 20° South.

Each degree of latitude is divided into 60 minutes, and each of these minutes represents one nautical mile. This distance is recognised and used all over the world.

Because the Earth is not perfectly round, a nautical mile measured at different points on the Earth's surface varies in length, but to make life easy it is usually taken as 6080 feet. This is somewhat longer than a land mile. A speed of one nautical mile (NM) per hour is called one *knot*, so if your cruising speed is 20 knots you will be travelling at well over 20 mph. If you measure

your route on the chart with dividers and check it against the latitude scale to find the distance, you can work out how long it will take you. Also, if you record the times when you pass charted objects, and know your speed and direction, you can work out roughly where you are.

### Direction

In enclosed waters you can often steer directly by visible landmarks or navigation marks. If you can identify these on the chart they provide ideal reference points. You can check the adjacent water for dangers and draw a 'clearing line' on the chart that clears them all, passes through your visible reference point and aligns with another visible feature. By keeping this 'transit' aligned as you drive, the boat will stay on track regardless of wind and tide, and stay away from the rocks and sandbanks.

➤ **If you can draw a line on the chart that clears all dangers and passes through two charted features, you can follow it on the water by visually aligning the marks. You can work out routes like this in advance.**

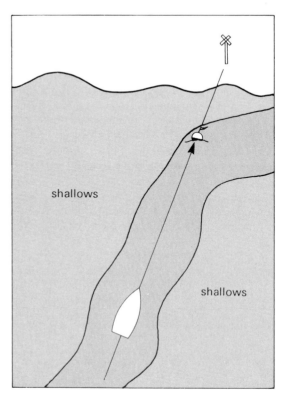

➤ **You can use a pair of dividers to measure off distance against the latitude scale up the side of the chart.**

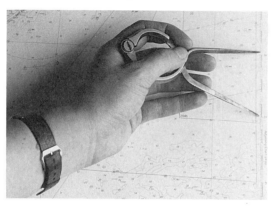

If you cannot find a visual alignment you will have to think in terms of compass bearings.

Somewhere on the chart you will find a large circle printed with degrees. This is the compass rose. The outer circle is the *true* compass rose, with north aligned on the north pole (and the vertical axis of the chart). The inner circle is the *magnetic* compass rose, with north aligned on *magnetic* north. This is different from the north pole (and varies according to where you are in the world) – but you need to know about it because it is the north indicated by your compass.

You may have two types of compass on board: a ship's compass and a handbearing compass. The ship's compass is mounted on the boat in front of the helm position, and you use it to steer by. So if you want to steer directly east you turn the boat until the ship's compass indicates 90° and head off in that direction, watching the compass all the time.

The handbearing compass is more interesting. You hold it in your hand, aim it at a visible mark such as a buoy, and take a note of the bearing. This is useful when you are trying to stay on track but cannot find a visual alignment for your reference point.

Assume you have drawn your clearing line on the chart, avoiding all dangers and passing through the position of a conspicuous buoy. Find the compass bearing of the line by comparing it with the *magnetic* compass rose on the chart. Then locate the buoy on the water (make sure it's the right one) and take its bearing with your handbearing compass. It will be different, so drive until it is the same and turn down the 'line'. Head towards the buoy, re-checking its bearing at intervals. That way you will stay on track.

Once you are on track you may be able to align the buoy with a conspicuous object on shore, such as a tree, and keep it aligned as you head towards it. An 'instant transit' like this saves a lot of re-checking with the compass, and is more accurate.

> If your clearing line passes through only one charted feature you will have to find its magnetic bearing, and stick to that bearing as you approach it on the water. In this case a tree comes into line with the buoy when you are on track, so if you keep it in line you will stay out of trouble, provided the buoy has not drifted off station.

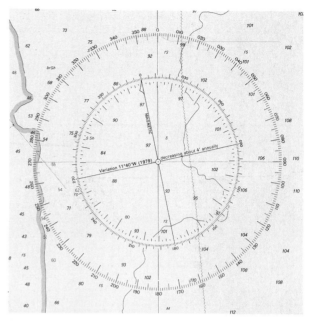

A compass rose from a chart, showing the inner 'magnetic' rose.

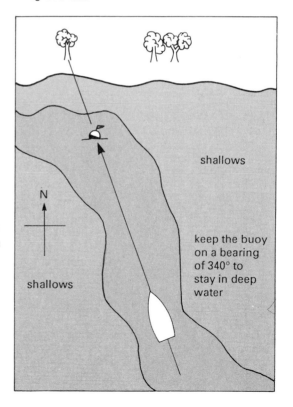

shallows

N

shallows

keep the buoy on a bearing of 340° to stay in deep water

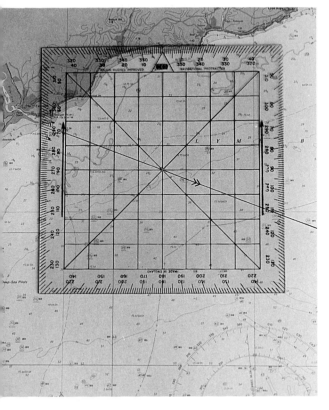

Plotting your position is easier if you use a Douglas Protractor, which is centred on the charted object and lined up with the chart grid. You then mark off the bearing using the degree scale inscribed round the edge. To use it you will have to convert your magnetic bearings into true bearings.

To use a handbearing compass, aim it at the object and read off the bearing.

### Position

Compass bearings and transits can also be used to fix your position. If you are very near a 'charted object' such as a buoy, then you know where you are on the chart. But what if the nearest buoy is some distance up an estuary, and you need to know where you are so that you do not hit the mud? You use the handbearing compass.

Aim the compass at the buoy and record the bearing. Find the bearing on the 'magnetic' compass rose on the chart and lay a ruler across it. Then find the buoy on the chart and draw a pencil line through the small circle at the base of the symbol, parallel to the ruler. (If possible, you should use parallel rules or a plotting device to ensure accuracy, but this is not always practicable in a fast open boat.)

Now look around for another visible object that is marked on the chart, such as a buoy, beacon or building. Take a bearing and draw a line. The two lines should cross at your position.

Unfortunately it is very hard to be accurate when you are doing this, so it is essential to take a bearing of yet another object as a check. If the line crosses somewhere near the others, forming a small triangle on the paper, you can be reasonably sure of your position. If not, something is wrong. Try again, using a fourth object if possible.

Transits are more accurate than compass bearings, so if you can see, say, a buoy and a lighthouse in direct alignment, draw a line through them on the chart and use this as one of your position lines.

However you use navigation marks, it is essential to identify them correctly. Always use binoculars to spot buoys, and check their features carefully against the information on the chart before you use them to fix your position.

Small powerboats are not really suitable for practising proper navigation techniques, but if you want to venture out to sea you should know something about them anyway. Read *Inshore Navigation* by Tom Cunliffe – also published by Fernhurst Books – for a readable, practical introduction to the subject. If you are aware of the problems you may encounter, you can work out your own ways of dealing with them. If you set off on a trip knowing nothing, you may never arrive.

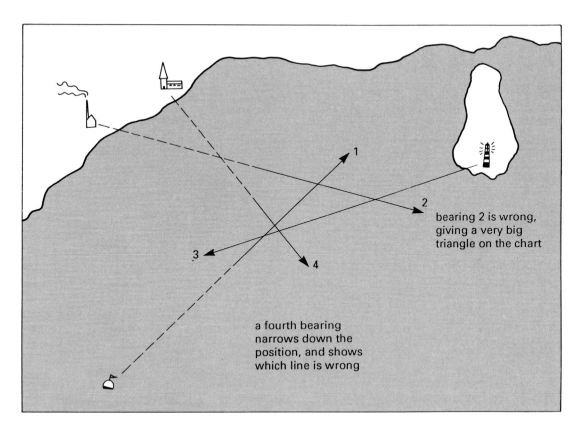

bearing 2 is wrong, giving a very big triangle on the chart

a fourth bearing narrows down the position, and shows which line is wrong

An ideal position fix is made up from three position lines that represent the compass bearings of three visible objects. The lines should converge on a small triangle. In this case the second bearing was wrong, but a fourth bearing showed up the error.

## PLANNING A CRUISE FOR A DAY

Flat, uninteresting coastlines do not encourage long trips, but if you tow your boat to an exciting holiday coast – or are lucky enough to live somewhere inspiring – you will want to explore it from the water. From first-hand experience of touring round the west coast of Scotland and the Outer Hebrides, I can recommend it as a magical experience. The wide open spaces and ever-changing moods of the water and weather are memories that will stay with me forever.

The golden rule with such a trip is NEVER ATTEMPT IT ALONE. In a small sportsboat you are ill-equipped and vulnerable. You need practical and moral support. Find some friends

who would like to venture further afield in their boats. Make up a small flotilla in this way or contact Club Committee members and ask them to organise a day or weekend trip. Pool your resources.

When you have made up your party, get together to pore over all the charts, tide tables and harbour information. For your first long trip, avoid being too ambitious. Work on the principle of small hops.

If the conditions allow you to travel at 20 knots, then it should take you one hour to travel 20 nautical miles. But this is not taking into account wind or tide, so it may well take longer. Check the forecast wind direction and strength, and try to plan the journey so that you are travelling into the wind. This is wetter and colder than travelling with it, but if the conditions worsen and you are forced to return home, this will ensure you have a reasonably soft, dry and warm return passage.

Use the chart to check for bolt holes – safe ports where you can dive for cover if the conditions deteriorate. You need to know the whereabouts of such places and how to enter them in safety. One of you might even be under tow with an engine down.

Radio communication between the craft is essential on both long and short hauls. Inform your friends on the shore (do not worry the coastguards, they are too busy) of the proposed route of the journey, expected time of arrival and how much time to allow before calling the rescue agencies if you do not appear. The rescue agencies will need to know the type of craft they are looking for, its name, colour, size and the number of people on board. They will also ask for details of equipment carried and the proposed route of the journey. (While you are looking on the black side, check your insurance cover for coastal trips.)

One member of the party should contact the person in charge at your proposed destination: the marina controller or harbourmaster. This is not purely a matter of courtesy; it ensures that you are made welcome and that there is sufficient room for your group to moor up or berth alongside a pontoon on your arrival. Ensure you can refuel and that the correct grade of fuel for your engine is available. Alternatively, you might be able to carry all your fuel with you.

Decide on a maximum wind strength for your smallest craft. You may decide to drop one and double up on another boat. Do not be tempted to take a friend's boat if it is unsuitable. Flexibility is the key to success.

Having planned a coastal hop in great detail, the most difficult decision is whether to cancel the venture because of threatened adverse weather conditions. A full-blown gale will not present a problem since everyone will be in agreement to give up the whole idea. The difficulty arises when there is a high wind predicted, but the day dawns bright and sunny with a light breeze blowing. The best advice here is: if in doubt, don't go to sea. Always have an alternative plan whereby you can enjoy each other's company on dry land.

◗ Before you set off, check the chart for ports of refuge, bearing in mind the probable wind direction. In this northerly gale the northern end of Dead Man's Bay would be well sheltered, but the wind howling into Cosy Cove could turn it into a deathtrap. If the wind backed round to the southwest the situation would be reversed.

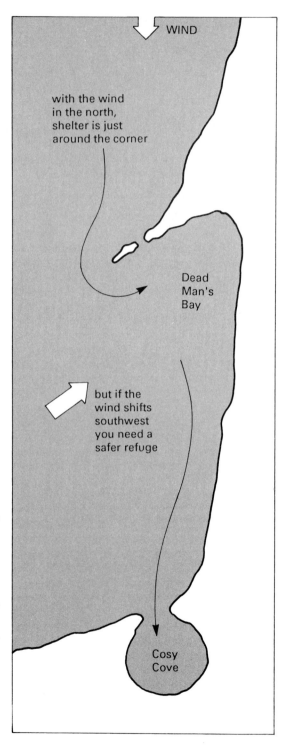

WIND

with the wind in the north, shelter is just around the corner

Dead Man's Bay

but if the wind shifts southwest you need a safer refuge

Cosy Cove

## Clothing

Always take waterproof coveralls or similar, together with spare warm clothes and towels all stowed in a waterproof kitbag. It can be wet and cold out there.

## Food

Eat well before embarking on such a journey but stay well clear of alcohol, which lowers your resistance to exposure. Carry hot drinks or soup in crush-proof heat retaining flasks or containers. Pack up a supply of sandwiches, fresh fruit, crisps, chocolate and fresh water, together with plastic cups and spoons. You can buy cans of stew that automatically heat the contents when needed; these do not require a cooker and are ideal for emergency rations.

## Personal

Having spent about two hours preparing the craft and supplies, do not forget about yourself. Pay a visit to the toilet before climbing into your wetsuit. Imagine how difficult it would be to relieve yourself in a fast open sportsboat when you are wearing several layers of clothing . . .

◀ **Wrap up well before you venture out to sea, and make sure your boat and engine are in good shape. Most importantly, never attempt a long trip alone, in one boat, for if something goes wrong you will have nothing to fall back on except the rescue services.**

## The journey

Move out into deep water and hug the coast, following your predetermined route and checking your bearings with known navigation marks or landmarks. Keep a weather eye open at all times, but do not motor too close behind other boats; travel in echelon formation, like geese in flight. Looking in the direction from which the weather is approaching. Adopt a speed that is comfortable for your boat and the other craft travelling with you. Maintain visual contact at all times, but do not motor too close behind other boats; travel in echelon formation, like geese in flight. When you are 20 minutes out, check that all the power units in the party are functioning properly.

You experience a wonderful euphoria at the completion of a successful trip which makes all the planning and organisation worthwhile. If you cover all the angles everything should go smoothly and you will learn a lot. Have a good day!

# 10 Man overboard!

This is a serious situation which should never arise and seldom does. However, you must know what to do about it, since this could mean the difference between life and death.

Ideally, of course, you should make sure it never happens, by avoiding all the following situations:

- Crew not secure before moving away.
- Accelerating too fast.
- Rough conditions.
- Travelling too fast for the conditions.
- Mechanical failure – usually steering controls – owing to poor maintenance.
- 'Messing about'.
- Striking another boat or sandbank.
- Incorrect approach to a mooring, jetty or pontoon.
- Sunbathing on the foredeck.
- Sitting on the bow, dangling feet in the waves.
- Changing over seating arrangements while underway.
- Crew very cold, leading to disorientation.
- Leaning over the side, being seasick.

➤ **Make sure the crew are seated while you are underway. This crew member is in a very vulnerable position and could fall overboard if the boat accelerates.**

Even if you take every precaution, you may still make a miscalculation one day and find yourself toppling over the side. If this happens to you, then:

1 Shout as you fall overboard. The crew will be looking forwards and might not notice you have disappeared.
2 Inflate your lifejacket.
3 Remain calm. You will be disorientated when you rise to the surface.
4 Check yourself over. Hitting the water at speed resembles an impact with a brick wall. Whatever happens, stay calm.
5 If cold, remain still and bring your knees up to the surface. Hold the inner sides of your arms tightly against the sides of your chest, with your hands down in your groin area, and keep your thighs pressed together. This position helps to minimise the loss of vital body heat.
6 If you are not wearing a lifejacket or buoyancy aid, then tread water, moving your arms and legs just enough to keep your head above water. Because of this limb movement you will lose body heat about one-third faster than if you keep still – as you could if you were wearing a lifejacket.

**7** Do not swim about or make for the shore. Remain in place and await the return of the boat. You will drift with the current, but when the boat comes alongside you and stops, it will also drift with the current while you prepare to get back on board.

## Boat crew

**1** As soon as the cry goes out 'Man Overboard', check astern and locate the position of the MOB. If possible, detail one member of the party to continually point at the MOB. If there were only two of you on board, you will have to keep the MOB in sight yourself.

**2** Regain control of the craft. Check the wind direction by noting the direction of the waves. Manoeuvre the craft into a wide circle and approach the MOB from downwind.

**3** Approximately 50 metres away from the MOB, reduce your speed to tickover and slowly approach into the waves, taking them on the bow. The MOB will be drifting in the waves towards you; aim to come alongside on the starboard side.

**4** Go into neutral and allow the weight of the boat to carry it over the last few metres. As soon as contact is made, SWITCH OFF THE ENGINE, for as soon as the MOB makes contact and holds onto the side of the boat, his legs will swing under the hull and down towards the propeller. If the engine is still switched on and in gear the consequences could be very nasty indeed. Use the paddle to manoeuvre the boat nearer the MOB if you stop too far away.

It is worth practising this with a dummy. A plastic drum half-full of water or an old tyre and lifejacket tied together will make the exercise as realistic as possible as far as weight goes. Man overboard practice improves boat handling skills, builds up confidence in the crew and goes some way towards preparing for an emergency. It can also be surprisingly good fun, so have a go.

▶ **If you lose a man overboard steer the boat round until you are well downwind of the casualty and then motor up towards him, facing directly into the wind. Ignore the tide, which will affect both the MOB and the boat in the same way. Switch the engine off as soon as you make contact.**

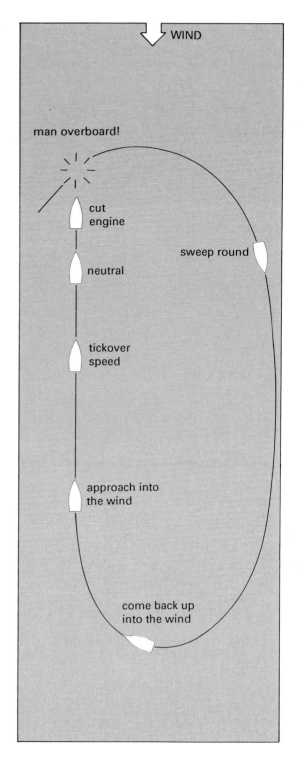

WIND

man overboard!

cut engine

neutral

sweep round

tickover speed

approach into the wind

come back up into the wind

🔺 **Man overboard!**

🔺 **Get the boat under control while avoiding the MOB.**

🔺 **Approach the MOB from directly downwind.**

🔺 **Slow down as you approach.**

🔻 **Never steer away from a man overboard since the stern – and the propeller – will swing towards him, and could easily kill him. Turn the wheel towards the MOB, and the stern will swing away from him.**

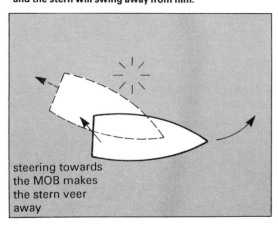

steering towards
the MOB makes
the stern veer
away

### Recovery: inflatable boat

Recovery into a rubber inflatable should be easy. Lift and roll the MOB over the side and inboard. If he is heavy and difficult to lift, then inflate his lifejacket (if worn) and, having first warned him of your intentions, turn him so his back is to the boat, place your hand on his head, force him under the water and release him. He will pop out of the water like a rubber ball, and you can catch him and lift him over the side and into the boat.

If he is injured, it may be possible to let some of the air out of one of the side tubes of the inflatable. This makes it easier to roll the injured person inboard. Your tool kit should include a pump so that you can replace the air in the tube after the recovery.

It is a good idea to keep ropes snap-shackled to the edge of the boat for use as grab handles.

▲ **Someone should keep pointing at the MOB.**

▲ **Turn the boat to get downwind. Keep pointing.**

▲ **Go into neutral when you get close.**

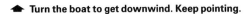

▲ **Cut the engine on contact.**

One of these can be dropped as a loop under the water for the MOB to stand in.

Recovery via the stern of the craft can be used with inflatables, as explained below.

### Recovery: solid hull

Approach the MOB on the starboard side, so you can maintain visual contact from the driver's seat. If you attempt a pick-up from the port side, you will lose sight of him for several minutes. Having made contact, use a rope to stop the MOB sliding along the smooth length of the hull.

Recovery over the side can be a problem in a small powerboat. If there are two of you left on board, and you both move to assist the MOB, your combined weight on one side of the boat could cause a capsize. To avoid this, use a stern recovery.

With the engine switched off, move the MOB to the stern of the boat and encourage him to use the anti-cavitation plate above the propeller as a step. If he is exhausted, you may have to use it yourself. Some rescue craft have a roll bar fitted at the stern to protect the crew if capsized in shallow water. A webbing strap attached to the bar will support you (or the MOB) while climbing over the stern.

Some powerboats have a bathing platform fitted to the stern, combined with a stainless steel ladder. This might appear to be the ideal recovery aid, but in practice the ladder does not always go deep enough into the water. The MOB has to kneel on the bottom rung and kneeling on a metal rod is painful. Fit some padding to the bottom rung: it makes the ladder more comfortable for bathers, too!

You should only attempt a stern recovery in a small boat or in fairly calm conditions. With a fairly large craft and a heavy sea, the stern and bow may lift high out of the waves before crashing back down. The stern would not be a safe place for anyone and trying to recover an MOB from this position could lead to serious, possibly fatal injury. Recover the MOB amidships, where the movement of the craft is at its minimum. Use a scrambling net, which does not take up much room when stowed on board.

**Problems: injured MOB**

The various methods of recovery discussed above are only practical if the MOB is able to assist. If he is injured or unconscious you have a problem. This is not so acute with an inflatable boat, since you can recover him by letting air out of one of the side tanks, but recovery into a solid-hull boat is much more difficult.

The first thing to do is secure the MOB to the side of the craft to stop him floating away. Then, if he is not wearing a lifejacket or personal flotation device (PFD), he must be fitted with one. This could mean that a second person has to enter the water.

Be cautious when making this decision. Carefully assess the situation, giving consideration to the following:
- Is the second person correctly dressed?
- Has he a lifeline attached?
- Would it be possible for the second person to return aboard without problems?
- Can he perform artificial respiration, if need be?
- Is he competent?
- Will the entering of the water by this second person put his own life at risk or put the remaining crew and boat at risk?

It is a difficult decision to make, and you need to make it fast. Personally, I try to avoid a second person entering the water.

**Problems: you need help**

The MOB is alongside, secure and floating with the aid of a lifejacket. He is breathing. But you

◀ Getting the MOB back aboard is hard work, even if there are two of you. The soft, low sides of this RIB make the job relatively easy; it is much harder with a high-sided sportsboat.

cannot get him into the boat. If you try to tow him ashore he could well slip into the propeller, the bow wave could drown him or, at the very least, the movement through the water will quickly drain away his body heat.

You need help, and speed is of the essence. You must attract the attention of other craft in the vicinity, by one of the following:

*Sound*    Whistle; foghorn; shouting.

*Visual*    Torchlight; slowly raising and lowering your arms while facing other boats.

*Radio*    Marine radio message to another vessel. They will need to know the name and colour of your vessel, and your position. Give your bearing FROM a charted object, and your approximate distance from it. To get the bearing, point your handbearing compass at an identifiable object such as a headland or lighthouse, take the bearing and either add or subtract 180° to come up with an answer between 0° and 360°. Alternatively, give a lat/long position if you know it.

*Flares*    Orange smoke if close to shore (3–4 miles); red rockets if offshore; red flare at night (3–4 miles).

Let us assume you make contact, and assistance is to hand. Bring the rescue boat alongside, but not on the side where the MOB is secured since it could squash him. Secure the two boats together and switch off all engines.

Your next move depends on the type of vessel that has come to your aid. If it is a small powerboat, you will simply benefit from the extra physical strength of its crew. A larger powerboat may have davits at the stern with a small boat hanging from them; use this to scoop the MOB from the water.

If a sailing yacht offers assistance this is fortuitous since yachts are fully equipped with excellent lifting tackle. You can use the mainsheet on the block and tackle at the end of the boom, tying the rope to the MOB's lifejacket. You can use a halyard intended for lifting a sail in much the same way, employing a winch to hoist the MOB out of the water and onto the yacht. Alternatively you may be able to drop a sail into the water, still attached to the top of the mast by the halyard, slide the MOB into the sail and winch him up, taking care that he is not injured on the stanchions as he is rolled inboard.

## NIGHT RESCUE

It is rare for sportsboats to be used at night, but if you are unlucky enough to lose someone in the dark, this is what you do:

1 Put the helm hard over to the same side as the MOB. Keep the helm hard over and the engine speed constant for an alteration of course of roughly 60° from the original heading.

2 Then put the helm over to the opposite lock and hold it there for a course change of approximately 210°. When you reach this course, cut the power and allow the boat to drift down to the MOB who should, by now, be directly ahead.

This method is one that has been recognised by users of larger craft and fishing boats for some considerable time now.

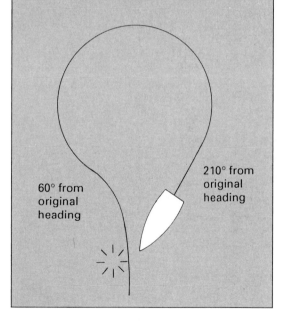

60° from original heading

210° from original heading

### In extremis

If there is no help nearby and you cannot get your casualty aboard, then you will have to resort to professional rescue services. The best way of summoning such help is by radio, and you should attend a course for the Certificate of Competence in handling VHF Radio. A recognised course in First Aid is also highly recommended.

# 11 Safety boat

Many people get their first taste of powerboating when they find themselves on the safety boat rota at their local sailing or canoe club. This is unfortunate, since the safety boat is no place for a beginner. If a dinghy or canoe gets into difficulties the safety boat will probably have to go to its aid – and may have to cope with people in the water, damaged craft, tangled lines that may foul the propeller, shallow water and, in the case of sailing dinghies, the high winds and heavy seas that probably caused the problem in the first place.

This type of situation demands good boat handling, resourcefulness, clear thinking and a knowledge of first aid. The scope for making mistakes is enormous, and it is not unknown for dinghy crews to refuse help from a scratch safety boat crew for fear of further damage or injury. This defeats the whole object of having a safety boat, so it is essential that all safety boat crews are properly trained in both basic boat handling and rescue techniques.

## SUITABLE BOATS

The term safety boat is often applied to the large displacement craft that accompany flotillas of dinghies or canoes and function as 'mother ships', carrying the spare gear, veteran club members and sandwiches. Such boats are really outside the scope of this book and, in any case, are not suitable for rescuing people in the water or salvaging damaged craft.

For this you need a small, fast boat with a low freeboard. A smart V-hulled sportsboat is not appropriate, since it lacks cockpit and storage space and is not particularly stable at low speeds. The ideal is a dory or a rigid-hulled inflatable.

A cathedral-hulled dory is excellent for inland waters. It provides a stable, roomy platform at rest, yet is fast and manoeuvrable up on the plane. At sea it is less satisfactory, for although very buoyant (owing to built-in buoyancy in the double-skinned hull) a dory is uncomfortable and

wet in big waves, and has a tendency to fill up and become awash.

For coastal work the best choice is a rigid-hulled inflatable: a fast, buoyant, roomy and stable craft that handles big waves well and has soft sides, making it very suitable for situations where contact with other boats and people is a frequent occurrence.

Both types of boat would normally be powered by an standard outboard motor, but in confined waters where high speed is less of a priority it might be worth considering a water-jet engine or shrouded propeller. This will minimise the risk of injury to people in the water, particularly in situations where the safety boat crew lack experience.

### RESCUE EQUIPMENT

In addition to the equipment listed on page 15 you should stow the following:
- Heaving lines (floating lines terminating in a soft weight or monkey's fist).
- Tow ropes in several lengths, for side tows, long tows and combination tows, each fitted with snap shackles at each end.
- Spare lifejackets.
- Spare clothing and waterproofs.
- Spare shackles, clevis pins, bungs and short lengths of twine suitable for quick repairs.
- A radio (VHF or CB) for contact with the shore base and other safety craft.

You should always have two people in the boat, if only to provide the musclepower to heave casualties out of the water. One person may need to manoeuvre the safety boat while the other rigs lines or even enters the water, or one crew member may have to perform first aid while the other steers for the shore.

▲ A rigid inflatable is the ideal craft for rescue work at sea. Buoyant, stable and fast, it is also extremely seaworthy in big seas.

## PEOPLE IN THE WATER

The technique for this is exactly the same as for recovering a man overboard (see Chapter 10), but it may be made easier by the fact that you are in total control at all times. On the other hand you may experience problems if the casualty is entangled in the running rigging of a capsized boat.

Approach into the wind, as if you were picking up a mooring buoy. Watch out for ropes in the water that could foul your propeller, and switch off the engine as soon as you make contact. Refer to Chapter 10 for recovery techniques.

## SAILING DINGHIES

A dinghy race on a gusty day can keep a safety boat crew very busy, so it is vital that you know where to be and what to do.

### Position
You must be able to attend any capsize within three minutes. If someone is lying face downwards in the water for longer he will suffer brain damage from oxygen deficiency, and will soon drown.

Because of this it is essential that you station yourself where the action is. In a sailing race,

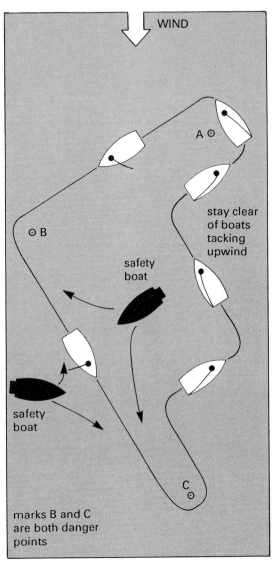

▲ An Olympic-style course for a dinghy race showing the accident-prone downwind legs to the gybe mark, and suitable places to station the safety boat.

most of the upsets occur on the downwind leg (when the dinghies are running before the wind), and as they gybe round the buoy at the end of the leg. However, it is a mistake to hold station downwind of the buoy on a windy day, since the wind and waves will impede you if you have to help someone. Try to stay upwind of any problem areas.

## Approaching capsized craft

Nine times out of ten the crew of a capsized dinghy will right it themselves, but you can never be sure. You should motor to within hailing distance and ask them if all is well. If they reply confidently do not interfere, but stand by, just within earshot, until they are up and sailing again. Meanwhile keep a good lookout for other casualties, and be prepared to shoot off to their aid. Remember the three-minute rule.

If you get no reply then they need help, fast. When the dinghy is on its side, approach the area forward of the mast. This will keep your propeller well clear of the crew in the water, and enable you to stop the mast sinking. If the mast has already sunk and the dinghy is fully inverted, come alongside with your bows pointing in the same direction. Always locate the crew first, and, if necessary, get them into the safety boat. When you are sure they are all right, you can consider salvaging their dinghy.

## Righting a capsized dinghy

If the dinghy crew are in good shape they will do most of the work themselves, but if you are stationed near the forestay you can help by lifting the mast. Alternatively you can come alongside the hull of the dinghy (be careful!) and use your crew weight to provide extra leverage on the dinghy centreboard.

It will help if you manoeuvre both craft round to face the wind; that way there is less wind pressure on the dinghy hull and sails, and less risk of the dinghy capsizing again on top of you.

▲ In light winds you can approach from upwind, aiming for the area forward of the mast. This keeps the propeller clear of the dinghy crew in the water.

▲ From this position you can lift the masthead. The crewman is standing on the centreboard (keel) to try and lever the mast out of the water.

▲ In strong winds it is safer to approach from downwind, since you are less likely to overrun the crew.

▲ Push the bows round into the wind, then bear down on the end of the centreboard to help right the boat.

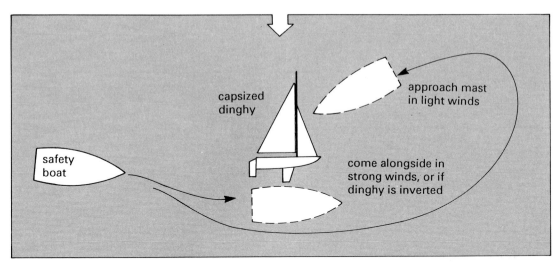

capsized dinghy

approach mast in light winds

safety boat

come alongside in strong winds, or if dinghy is inverted

▲ 'Walk' the mast up to unstick the sail from the water and help the boat right itself.

▲ Once the sail is clear of the water the dinghy will come up fast. The crewman has to climb in rapidly to stop the boat flipping on top of him.

▲ Try to control the boat as it comes up, or it may flip right over on top of you. This can be painful . . .

▲ Check that the crew have their boat sorted before you leave them to it.

 If the dinghy is completely inverted, prepare a long line and pass one end to the crewman, who should tie it to the shroud on the far side of the boat.

🔺 Secure your end of the line and reverse slowly. Always pull directly abeam to pull the mast out of the bottom if it is stuck there.

## Righting an inverted dinghy

If a dinghy flips right over it will often end up with its mast stuck in the bottom. This makes recovery awkward, because it is quite easy to snap the mast.

In deep water the mast will be free. You should come alongside and press down on the back of the boat on the windward side to bring it up to the normal capsize position. If this fails, take a jibsheet over the dinghy, stand on the opposite side and pull. If you attach the jibsheet to a long line (use a sheet bend) you can use the power of the safety boat to pull the dinghy up. Alternatively you could clip the long line to the base of a shroud. Always pull directly in line with the mast, so as to extract the masthead from the bottom if it is stuck there.

Once you have the dinghy on its side you can continue as for a normal capsize.

## TOWING

If the dinghy (or any other boat) is disabled you may have to tow it ashore. There are three basic ways of doing this.

### Long tow

Manoeuvre upwind or uptide of the disabled boat, so that it tends to drift away from you, and throw a heaving line to the crew. Make sure it is attached at your end! Ask them to tie their painter (bow line) to the heaving line while you attach your end to a strong towing point.

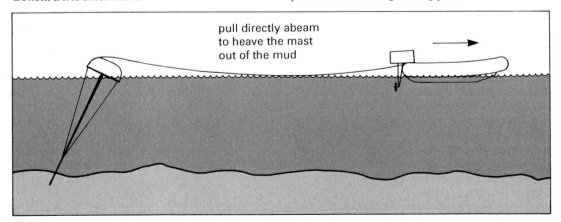

pull directly abeam
to heave the mast
out of the mud

▲ As the mast comes up you can either carry on as for a normal 180° capsize, or carry on pulling to draw the boat completely upright.

▲ Once the boat is upright you can retrieve the line. As before, check all is well before leaving the dinghy crew to get their boat going again.

When the ropes are joined, ask the other crew to sit near the stern of their boat to lift the bow. If their boat is overloaded, pull them alongside and transfer some of their crew to your boat. The raised bow will stop the boat yawing as it is towed.

Motor off gently to take up the slack, and tow the boat home at displacement speed. If you are travelling into the waves all will be well, but if the waves are overtaking you they will tend to push the towed boat forward, putting slack in the tow-rope and possibly fouling your propeller. Prevent this by asking the towed crew to drag a makeshift sea anchor such as a loop of rope or a bucket. This will slow them down and keep the tow-rope taut.

➤ You can tow a dinghy with a long line secured around the mast, and lashed to the forestay for stability (see inset). Tie your end to a strongpoint or a strop rigged across the stern.

## Stern tow

A sailing dinghy can be awkward to tow, because it tends to yaw about as it skims along on its flat stern sections. One way round this is to tow it stern-first, so that its V-shaped bow cuts the water and keeps it in line. With some dinghies you can do this at planing speed for a quick recovery.

Remove and stow the sails, rudder assembly and centreboard. Place a long line around the mast and shrouds, pass it under the boat to the stern and tie it off. Attach the towline to the tie of this girdle and to the thwart or mast of the dinghy.

Allow a reasonable length of towline and drive away. The pull on the stern of the dinghy will lift it and its bow will drop. Try accelerating onto the plane. The dinghy should plane backwards. If it is unhappy, slow down and continue at displacement speed.

## Side tow

Draw alongside the disabled craft (with your fenders out), and position your stern a short distance behind theirs. Take your painter and attach it to the stern of the disabled boat. Make sure it is secure, since this is the rope that takes most of the strain. Use two smaller lines to hold the bow and stern of each boat together. If the disabled boat has an outboard engine, lift it to reduce drag.

Once you are underway, make sure the stern of your boat stays well behind the stern of the other, since this allows you to steer effectively. If you have to go astern, attach an additional line running from the bow of the disabled craft to your stern.

◆ **You can sometimes tow a dinghy stern-first at planing speed, since the V-hulled bow holds it in line.**

◆ **When side-towing, ensure that the towed boat is lashed ahead of yours for maximum manoeuvrability.**

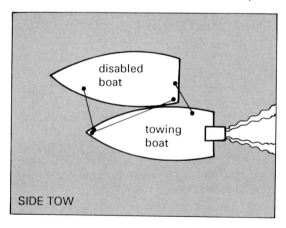

SIDE TOW

## SAILBOARDS

It can be hard to know when a boardsailor is in trouble. To the casual observer he may appear to be in trouble most of the time! Normally he will just haul up the rig and carry on, but repeated dunkings will take their toll. Sooner or later he will get tired, and once this happens he may not be able to get back to the shore unaided.

Another problem is visibility. Since both the board and rig lie flat on the water when not under way, it is easy to miss them among waves.

Safety boat crews involved in board racing events should be able to spot a boardsailor with a problem before he has to signal for help. By the time he gets to that stage he may be too cold and exhausted to call or wave. If possible, the safety boat should be manned by people who are themselves active in boardsailing and know the difference between someone suffering a temporary setback and someone in distress. Such people will also know how to de-rig a board quickly without damaging it.

The type of boat also needs consideration. A safety boat with a high freeboard is useless, since the high sides make it almost impossible to tow the board home. On inland waters an inflatable is ideal, but it should be at least four metres long with a solid floor. At sea, use a rigid-hulled inflatable.

## Approach

A drifting board will tend to swing round so that the mast points into the wind while the 'hull' drifts downwind. In light winds, the quickest approach is to arrive at the masthead with the safety boat heading in the same direction as the board. The rig can then be pulled across the safety boat and the sailor brought aboard. Be sure to cut the engine as soon as you make contact, if not before, since the impact may knock the sailor into the water.

In stronger winds this is dangerous, because you may override the board. Approach from downwind and come up alongside with your bows pointing in the same direction. Cut the engine immediately and transfer the sailor to the boat.

◂ **In light winds approach a sailboard from the masthead, with your boat pointing the same way as the board (left). Haul the rig over the back of the boat (centre) and get the sailor aboard (right).**

◂ **In stronger winds it is safer to approach from downwind, but this makes recovering the board itself rather more awkward.**

If he is cold, he should sit in the bottom of the boat out of the wind. If he is injured or suffering from hypothermia, administer first aid and get him ashore, leaving someone else to take care of the board.

## Board recovery: inshore

If your boardsailor is in good shape, he will want you to recover his board immediately. You do this by holding the rig across the safety boat and driving away with the board itself in the water alongside.

When you approach from the masthead end this is fairly simple. Bring the sail across the boat until the board is close alongside, get the sailor into the boat and ask him to hold the mast firmly with the boom either inside or outside the hull. If the boat is very small he should sit in the bow to keep the rig clear of the helm. Raise the daggerboard and motor off.

**You can tow a sailboard ashore by holding the rig across the stern of the safety boat.**

If you approached from downwind the recovery is less easy. Getting the sailor aboard is no problem, but manoeuvring the rig across the safety boat from its upwind position can be an awkward business. A fully-battened rig can be particularly cumbersome; be careful the sail does not flip over in the wind and hit you.

If you have a big safety boat you may be able to stow both the board and its rig inside the boat. This enables you to head for the shore at speed. Conversely, with a small safety boat it may be better to separate the rig and board, and tow the board behind on a long towline. You will probably need to attach the towline to the board with a length of thin line through the towing eye.

If you pick up a boardsailor some distance from the coast, recovery without de-rigging is not practical. With some sails you can remove the sail battens, outhaul line and boom, and roll the sail towards the mast. More advanced fully-battened rigs will need to be completely dismantled by detensioning the battens, releasing all lines, removing the boom and sail, and rolling the sail in line with the battens. A good working knowledge of sailboard rigs is very helpful here.

## CANOES

Canoes are easier to deal with than dinghies or sailboards, since there is no rig to impede you. This means that you can always approach from the safest direction, motoring up into the wind/ tide as if you were picking up a mooring. Always

approach rafted canoes this way, as well as individual canoeists or casualties in the water, and ensure that any passengers embark or disembark near the bow, well away from the propeller.

Follow the man overboard drill for picking up a casualty. If he is in bad shape administer first aid and take him ashore immediately.

Once you have dealt with the canoeist you can return for his craft. Approach into the wind/tide as before and retrieve it with the boathook, being careful not to damage it. Then tow it ashore, either with a long line or, for short distances, by simply holding on to the bow. If it is swamped, you can empty it by bringing it alongside and tilting it onto its side, lifting it gently at each end. Never lift one end of the canoe and attempt to drag it inboard, or you will break its back.

## FIRST AID

Everyone who operates a powerboat should have some knowledge of first aid, but it is essential for safety boat crews. The main risks are drowning, loss of body heat, injury and shock; therefore the main elements of first aid on the water should be training in resuscitation, combating hypothermia, treating wounds and treating for shock. The aims are:
1 To preserve life.
2 To prevent the condition getting worse.
3 To promote recovery.
To this end, you should give treatment in the following order:
1 Breathing.
2 Bleeding.
3 Shock.

### Resuscitation
A casualty who has stopped breathing will suffer brain damage and die in a matter of minutes. To save him, you must use mouth-to-mouth resuscitation.
1 Shout at the victim and shake him – he may respond. Meanwhile call for help, using the radio if you are in the boat.
2 Get the victim into the boat. If you find this difficult get into the water, hold onto the boat and support his neck with your arm.

**3** Tilt the victim's head right back with the palm of your hand and lift his chin with your other hand. This will pull his tongue clear of the airway. Check for other obstructions such as mud or weed and clear them out.

**4** This may be enough to start him breathing. Look at his chest, listen, and hold your cheek close to his mouth to feel his breath. If he is breathing, put something under his shoulders so that his head falls back naturally to keep the airway open and get medical aid.

**5** If he does not start breathing, pinch his nose with the hand holding his forehead. Take a lungful of air, place your mouth over the victim's to make a seal and blow long and slow, as if you were inflating a large balloon.

**6** His chest should rise. If not, the airway must be blocked. Make sure his head is far enough back and his chin raised high enough. Try again. Check for obstructions. If he is unconscious and you suspect an obstruction roll him towards you and strike him four times between the shoulder blades with the heel of your open hand. Watch his mouth after each blow for signs of his throat clearing. Remove any debris from his mouth and try another inflation, watching for his chest to rise.

**7** Take away your mouth. The victim's chest should collapse again, pushing your air back out. If he has inhaled water this will rush out too; turn his head and clear this out.

**8** Turn his head back and repeat the long slow blow. Remove your mouth, release his nostrils and check to see if he is breathing. If not, continue with one breath every five seconds for an adult, or one every four seconds for a child, until he recovers or medical help arrives.

**9** When the victim begins to breathe on his own, place him in the recovery position. He will probably be sick, and if he is left on his back he may choke and stop breathing again. Keep watch, and keep his mouth clear.

When you call for help, you should get someone to send for an ambulance. If there are two of you in the boat – as there should be – and you have the victim on board, one of you should drive steadily for the shore, ideally to a point with road access, while the other continues with resuscitation. Make sure your radio contact knows where you are going.

◄ The author in the recovery position after reading his publishing contract. His knee and arm will stop him rolling over, and this will keep his airway clear if he is sick. If he was lying on his back he might choke – a common cause of death after a near-drowning.

### Injuries

If the patient is wet the water will spread the blood and make the injury look worse than it really is. Remember this and try not to look alarmed. Smile at the patient and reassure him. He will probably be suffering from shock, and you do not want to make it worse. If the wound is obviously serious, get medical aid, via the radio if you are on the boat.

The first priority is to stop the bleeding. If the cut is clean apply pressure: first with your fingers, and then using a clean, dry pad if you have one. If not, use anything handy.

If the wound is dirty cleanse it with the fresh water carried on board the safety boat and apply a pad. Do not apply pressure if there is a foreign body lodged in the wound: it will simply make matters worse. Do not remove the foreign body; simply protect the wound and seek help. If an arm or leg is injured, elevate the limb to reduce the blood flow. If the bleeding is bad restrict it by applying pressure to the nearest pressure point. These are located on the inner leg near the groin, and on the inner arm near the armpit.

### Shock

Shock is dangerous in its own right. Its effect is to increase the whole body's demand on its blood supply, which cannot cope; the brain and vital organs go short, and could suffer damage. The patient will look pale and his breathing will be shallow. He needs warmth and reassurance.

1 Speak calmly to him and reassure him. Look cheerful. It is important that he does not see you looking worried.

2 Ensure that he is lying comfortably on his back or side. Raise his legs. Handle him gently at all times.

3 Protect him from wind and spray, and wrap him up to conserve his body heat.

4 Moisten his lips, but do not give drinks. DO NOT GIVE ALCOHOL OR STIMULANTS.

5 Obtain medical help.

If a victim fails to respond to resuscitation, his rescuer will be in shock. Treat him accordingly. Even if the original victim recovers, the rescuer's elation at having saved a life may be too much for his system. Watch out for this. Rescue can be a traumatic business for all concerned.

## Hypothermia

The human body has a built-in thermostat that maintains its temperature at 37.2°C (98.6°F). An increase or decrease of only a few degrees at the body core can be fatal. In cold conditions the thermostat conserves heat by closing down the supply of warm blood to the extremities, which may go numb as a result. This is usually enough to preserve the core temperature above 35°C, but if not the victim's body heat will gradually ebb away until he dies. This is a very real possibility when someone has been in the water for some time. The symptoms will follow this pattern:

1 complaints of feeling cold
2 skin becomes abnormally cold
3 shivering violently
4 shivering decreases
5 no muscle co-ordination, slurred speech
6 comprehension dulled
7 irrational behaviour
8 pulse and respiration slow down
9 unconsciousness and death

### SURVIVAL TIMES

Survival time in cold water depends on the water temperature, air temperature, the victim's age, weight, health and fitness, and the efficiency of his protective clothing. It will be reduced if he has been drinking alcohol. The following are rough survival times.

| Water temperature (°C) | Survival |
|---|---|
| 15 | 3 hours |
| 10 | 2 hours |
| 5 | 90 minutes |

If the patient is still shivering he will probably be fine as long as you keep him warm. If he has gone beyond that, take him ashore immediately. On the way, try to prevent any further heat loss as follows:

1 Warm him up by covering his body, head and neck, but not his face. Do not remove wet clothing if you are out in an open boat; just add extra clothes. Alternatively, place him in an exposure bag, thermal blanket or even a dustbin liner. You should have these on board a safety boat. Consider asking someone warm to climb into the bag with him.

2 If he is unconscious, place him in the recovery position.

3 If conscious, offer a warm drink (if you have one) BUT NOT ALCOHOL.

Do not encourage exercise and do not rub or massage him. This will encourage warm blood away from his body core, where he needs it. Similarly, if you have access to a warm bath on shore, do not simply dump him in it; keep his arms and legs out of the warm water to retain the warm blood at the body core.

# 12 Problems

If you keep your boat and engine well maintained you can be reasonably confident that they will not let you down. But even the best-maintained craft run into problems occasionally, so it's as well to be prepared.

## BROKEN DOWN

If your engine stops you could be in real trouble. You need to keep calm and assess the situation coolly and constructively.

### Preliminary considerations
- Where are you?
- What is the risk?
- Where are you going to end up?
- Why have you broken down?

If you cannot re-start the engine after three attempts you may be a long time finding the problem. Meanwhile the drifting boat will swing sideways and roll with the waves in a most uncomfortable fashion, and you need to do something to steady it up.

### Sea anchor
A sea anchor is basically a drogue that slows wind-blown drift and pulls the bow into the waves. Use anything that will slow down the boat from the bow. This could be one of the following:
- A canvas bucket
- A chunk of rope
- An anchor
- A small 'sea parachute' designed for the job

Whatever you use, the purpose is the same: to keep the stern downwind and prevent waves swamping the boat.

Once you have steadied up the boat, check through the troubleshooting section (see page 88). If you still have no success at re-starting the engine, you will need to signal for assistance. This is the test of a comprehensive equipment list.

▶ **Raising and lowering your arms is a recognised distress signal. Never use it simply to attract the attention of your friends.**

### Radio signals
Try the VHF radio. You can ask for a tow from a nearby boat, or explain your problem to the coastguard. You may even get advice on re-starting your engine. In any event, you will know that other people are aware of your predicament.

If your radio is dead (always test it before every trip) then you will have to try some other method of attracting attention.

### Visual signals
- Lowering and raising your arms, outstretched to each side.
- Flash light: a sequence of three short, three long and three short flashes (SOS).
- Flares (but these should only be used if you are drifting into imminent danger of sinking or loss of life).

### Sound signals
There may be someone within shouting distance, but this will only work if they are downwind. For a more penetrating sound signal, you could try any of the following:
- The foghorn
- A bell note
- A whistle
- Gun shots, or an explosion (be careful!)

## TROUBLESHOOTING: OUTBOARDS

A handpull start on an outboard engine should be successful by the third attempt. If it isn't, then something is amiss. Don't simply keep pulling at it: continual pulling for ten minutes or so could easily result in the breakdown of the ignition unit and a costly replacement. Leave it alone and go through the following:

### Fuel
- Have you any fuel?
- Is it turned on?
- Has the bulb in the fuel line been primed? (You should feel a resistance when it is squeezed.)
- Is it connected from the petrol tank through to the engine?
- Has the top cap of the fuel tank been released to allow air into the tank when the fuel is taken out?
- Is the kill switch fitted? The engine will not – or should not – start without it.
- Is the fast idle lever or throttle control in the correct start-up position?

### Electric start
If the engine has an ignition-key start, you will need to push the ignition key in as you turn it to bring in the automatic choke.

If it is fitted with a push-button start, it will probably have a separate switch for the choke.

The engine will need choke until it fires. As soon as it fires, take off the choke control and it should run fast. Set the tick-over at about 1500 rpm and warm it up for three minutes.

If you have checked the choke and the engine still will not go, check the plugs.

### Plugs
Remove the plugs (make sure you have a plug spanner in your tool kit) and check them for oil. Sniff them: they should smell of petrol. Clean them and check the ignition gap, or replace the plugs with new ones.

If the engine still does not fire, you will have to get it looked at by a qualified engineer.

### Cooling system
Even if the engine starts, this does not mean that all is well. If the cooling system is not working, the engine will run perfectly for a while, then overheat and seize up.

On an outboard, the cylinder block is cooled by water pumped up from an inlet in the lower leg assembly, under the cavitation plate. Because the impeller of the pump uses water as its lubricant, an outboard engine must never be run out of the water unless water is supplied to the water inlet through a muff connected to a hose pipe.

When an engine is ticking over, there should be a jet of water emerging from somewhere below the engine cover as an indication that all is well. This outlet is a narrow tube which can easily become blocked by mud, seaweed or, over a period of time, by small marine animals. If this appears to be the case, try pushing a thin wire up inside the tube to clear the blockage. If you try this and still there is no water jet, close down the engine and have it serviced. If you continue to run the engine you risk destroying it. Much the same goes for inboard engines that are cooled by external water. Check your engine manual.

### Propeller and gearbox
If the engine is running well but you are getting no propulsion, there may be a fault with the propeller or gearbox. Try the following checks and tests:

- Switch off the engine and check the propeller. It is held in place by a washer, lock nut and split pin. If this lock nut is not secured correctly, the propeller can fall off. Has it? If so, do you carry a spare lock nut, split pin and propeller?

- If you can turn the propeller on the shaft by hand when the engine is in gear, check the shear pin or rubber compression bush. The shear pin is a small, soft metal pin, which snaps if something jams the propeller. Small engines up to 4 hp are usually fitted with shear pins, while modern, larger engines are generally fitted with a rubber compression bush which is designed to slip if the propeller jams and prevent damage to the gearbox.

- Check the gear-change mechanism. This can work loose and become disconnected from the gear box, in which case moving the gear lever back and forth will have no effect.

- With the engine off, move the gear lever into forward or reverse gear. Apply gentle pressure to the propeller. This should be locked and unable to move. If it does move, and feels rough and lumpy, the gearbox should be checked for internal damage. (Do not exert so much pressure on the propeller that it turns when in gear. Engines have been known to fire up and remove a hand.)

**Changing a propeller**

If you damage your propeller you will have to remove it from the engine and replace it. This is a fairly simple operation which can sometimes be carried out at sea using a pair of pliers, screwdriver, spanner, hammer and block of wood – assuming you carry a spare propeller! Make sure you do.

Propellers are also removed for security reasons, since they are a favourite target for thieves. If you have to leave your boat unattended in the boat park it makes sense to take the propeller off before someone else does. Here's how you do it:

1 Take a look at the locking nut. If it is a 'castle' nut held in place by a split pin, squeeze the splayed ends of the pin together with pliers and withdraw it.

2 If the nut is locked in place by a tab washer, lever the tabs out of their grooves with a screwdriver. Use a piece of wood to protect the cavitation ring of the propeller.

3 When all the locking tabs are released (or the split pin has been removed) undo the nut with a spanner. Wedge the propeller against the cavitation plate with the block of wood to stop it rotating, and possibly damaging the gearbox.

4 If the shaft is regularly greased the propeller should now come off. If not, hold your block of wood behind the propeller and hit the wood with a hammer until the propeller comes free.

5 Take the propeller off, being careful not to lose the thrust ring which stops it screwing itself through the gearbox.

6 Grease the shaft with recommended biodegradable grease. Reverse the sequence to refit the propeller.

▲ This propeller is held on by a split pin and castle nut. Remove the split pin with pliers.

▲ Undo the nut. A socket wrench is ideal, since the nut is recessed within the cavitation ring.

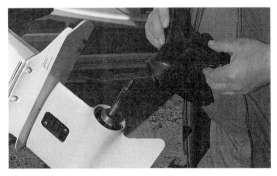

▲ Remove the propeller. It should come off easily; if not, the spindle needs re-greasing.

▲ Be careful not to lose the thrust ring at the back of the propeller.

## Bleeding a diesel to remove air

You should know how to remove air from a diesel fuel system because you might need to do so at sea. The following is a quick but messy method of doing so. Ensure the tool kit contains tools to fit all fuel line connectors and take the following steps:

**1** Slacken off all nuts connecting the system, by a half to a full turn. Leave them slack.

**2** Slacken off the filter and lift pump.

**3** Slacken off the fuel distribution pump.

**4** Slacken off the backs of the injectors.

**5** Crank over the engine, using the ignition key or start button. As the engine turns, it will pump and draw diesel through the system. The engine might start up. Let it run. Diesel will squirt out but, at worst, it will make a mess. It cannot catch fire.

**6** With the engine running, or cranking over, start at the fuel tank and re-tighten all the nuts, working towards the injectors on the engine. Always work in sequence, from the tank to the engine. When you have finished, there should be no air in the system.

**7** Clear up the mess, removing any spilt diesel.

## Salvaging a drowned engine

If your engine comes off the boat, or is swamped, the circumstances surrounding the accident will determine whether it will restart. Generally speaking, if the engine was running at speed when immersed, water will have been taken into the cylinder head through the carburettor. Unlike air which compresses, water does not reduce its volume under pressure, and the engine will seize up. However, if you are able to recover the engine from the water quickly after a swamping, it is worth trying the following:

**1** Check that the fuel has not been contaminated by the water.

**2** Remove the drain plugs on each of the carburettors and prime the fuel system until all the water and dirt is removed, leaving neat petrol flowing out. Replace the drain plugs on the carburettors.

**3** Remove all spark plugs and turn the engine over. There should be minimal resistance and the engine should turn over easily. At this point you will know whether there is a chance of the engine restarting. If a large quantity of water was taken into the cylinders at speed, the engine will have seized and will not turn. It will need to be rebuilt.

**4** If the engine turns, it should push any water and dirt out of the plug holes of the cylinders.

**5** Give a quick squirt of water displacement oil into each pot.

**6** Replace the plugs. Check the fuel system is primed.

**7** Liberally apply water displacement oil over the entire engine.

**8** Return to the normal starting procedure and re-start the engine.

➤ **If you have an outboard, make sure it is securely clamped to the back of the boat. This engine is also equipped with a security lock system.**

➤ **Always rig a safety line from the outboard to a strongpoint. Then if the clamps fail and engine goes overboard you may be able to salvage it.**

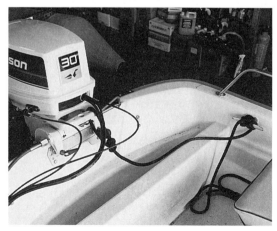

# 13 Maintenance and storage

The best way to deal with problems is to avoid them, by ensuring that you maintain the boat well and store it properly at the end of the season. The most basic element of maintenance is the daily routine after recovering the boat from the water.

## WASH DOWN

Use fresh water to wash down the hull and trailer. Then connect the engine muff to the hose-pipe, attach it to the cooling water inlet and turn on the tap. Fire up the engine. All the salt water, sand and mud will be washed out of the cooling system. With outboards, remove the fuel line and allow the engine to run dry. This prevents the oil residue being left in the carburettors when the petrol evaporates. Over a period of weeks, this oil can clog the jets and make the engine difficult to start.

If you follow this routine religiously it should keep the engine in good shape all season. However, there is more to maintenance than simply flushing out the system after every trip.

## BASIC CARE OF OUTBOARD ENGINES

The whole engine needs to be kept clean and dry. WD40 is often used for the displacement of water from the electrics and moving parts, but it should be used sparingly because, as it dries, it hardens. Excessive use of WD40 builds up a yellow skin over the engine surface, and this can cause the high-power electrical current to leak away. The water displacement oil sold for marine engines is recommended. This does the same job as WD40, but leaves a thin film of oil which does not dry.

Periodically wash down the whole engine using engine de-greasing gunk and then a solution of a soap-based washing up liquid.

▶ **Remove the engine cover and spray the works with marine water displacement oil after every trip. This will prevent corrosion.**

This also leaves a very thin oily film behind when it dries.

### Paintwork
Look after the engine paintwork. Wash it down with fresh water and a soap-based washing-up liquid, and retouch any scars with zinc chromate paint. The engine and covers are made of aluminium, and this has an electrolytic action when exposed to salt water which will destroy it.

### Grease
Use the grease specified by manufacturers. This will be bio-degradable and will not react to salt water.

### Gearbox oil
The gearbox has its own oil. It has a drain plug and a filler plug. Always use the oil recommended by the manufacturer and change as necessary. When changing the oil, note whether it looks 'milky' in colour. If it does, this means that salt water has seeped in through a loose seal and the gearbox needs servicing.

### Two-stroke oil
Two-stroke engines require oil mixed with the fuel to lubricate the engine. Use the recommended oil and mix it to the correct

⬆ It is essential to flush out the engine with fresh water after every session. Connect the hosepipe to the water inlet using the engine muffs, turn off the fuel, fire up and let the engine run until it stops.

proportions. Large engines usually work on a 50:1 mix of fuel to oil. With many engines you simply fill an oil reservoir, and the engine mixes it automatically. Do not use the two-stroke oil used for motorbikes and mowing machines, since it does not burn at the correct temperature and can dramatically reduce the life of the engine.

Most Japanese two-stroke engines will operate on low-octane or unleaded fuel, but the majority of American engines prefer medium grade. Check the octane rating of the fuel against the engine specifications.

### Fuel system

Cleanliness of the fuel system is essential. Prevent sand, dirt and water from entering the fuel tank. Keep fuel lines clean and in good order Use an in-line fuel filter to remove water.

## BASIC CARE OF INBOARD ENGINES

Similar treatment is recommended for inboard engines. De-gunk and wash down with a soap-based washing-up liquid. Use a watering-can, and pump out the bilge. Dry the engine and spray it with water displacement oil.

### Petrol (gasoline)

Petrol inboards are similar to car engines and require similar servicing:

- Ensure that the petrol filters are regularly changed.
- Check that the engine is always pumping cooling water.
- Check oil levels.
- Check the water level, if a heat exchanger is fitted, and remember to add anti-freeze for the winter (not necessary in warm climates). Make sure the anti-freeze is suitable for aluminium engine heads and heat exchangers.

### Diesel

- Change the filters on the fuel line regularly to remove dirt. There should be at least two filters on the system.
- Check the water separator in the fuel line. There is usually one. Water is heavier than diesel and collects in a bowl at the bottom near a drain-off tap or screw. This needs to be released from time to time to remove the water.
- Check the level of the engine oil, and change it at the recommended intervals.
- Check the level of the gearbox oil, and change it at the recommended intervals. Always use the oil specified by the manufacturer.
- Check that the engine is pumping cooling water.
- Check the water level in the heat exchanger unit, if fitted, and make sure it contains an anti-freeze solution of the right type.

## RUNNING-IN AND FIRST SERVICE

A new engine should have been given a P.D.I. (Pre-Delivery Inspection). Check with the dealer to ensure that this has been carried out. It will also have a recommended running-in period, with a time-scale regarding the running-in speeds. Adhere to this.

During this period, or at the end of it (between 20 and 50 hours), the first service will be due. This is the most important service of all, and will set up the engine for the rest of its life. A good marine engineer will virtually strip and rebuild the engine and then run it up in a test tank. As with a car, it will need to be serviced again at regular intervals, the frequency of which depends upon the future use of the engine and the hours logged.

## STORAGE (WINTERISATION): OUTBOARDS

The engine should be fully serviced at the end of the season. This means it should be stripped down completely, cleaned, rebuilt and retested.

Having had this done, drain all the fuel out of the fuel system and squirt 'storage seal' into the plug holes and carburettors. This resembles white shaving cream and prevents fuel and oil gelling up in the combustion chambers. It also stops condensation and rusting within the bore (bigger engines have chromed bores, and moisture will lift the chrome.)

A quicker method is to warm up the engine and, while it is running, squirt marine two-stroke oil into the carburettor air inlets. Then remove the fuel line. While the engine is burning off the fuel in the system the whole inside of the engine oils up and will be protected. This is less effective than storage seal, but better than nothing.

Drain out the fuel tanks and turn them upside down with the tops off. This prevents a build-up of water and the resultant rust. It is worth noting here that the modern additives in petrol (gasoline) break down after about three months and the fuel goes stale, as well as attracting moisture. Any old fuel left in an outboard system will cause running problems for the engine. Always dispose of old fuel safely: do not pour it into ditches or down drains. Think of the environment and seek advice on suitable methods of disposal.

Remove the battery from the boat and put a car spotlight across the connections to drain the battery flat. The battery will store better this way. Alternatively, store it in a dry place and recharge it monthly.

### Recommissioning

At the beginning of the new season recharge the battery, refuel the system and fire up the engine in a water tank or with the engine muffs connected to a hose pipe. Always turn the water on first, and never exceed 1500 rpm.

The storage seal will burn off after a few starts. Clouds of smoke will pour out and the plugs might oil up and need cleaning. Persevere. Within a short time the engine should be running smoothly.

## WINTERISATION: INBOARD DIESELS

Manufacturers will have their own recommended programmes for engine storage, but if you have no information you should try the following.

Before removing the craft from the water:

1 Start the engine and warm it up. This makes the oil more fluid.

2 Stop the engine and drain off the engine oil.

3 Replace the sump plug and refill with recommended anti-corrosion oil to the bottom mark on the oil dipstick.

4 Mix two litres of diesel fuel with one litre of recommended anti-corrosion oil in a clean container.

5 Disconnect the fuel line and hold the end of the fuel line hose in this container. Start up the engine and run it for 10–15 minutes, then close it down.

With the craft out of the water, take the following steps. (Note that there are two types of cooling system: the engine may use a closed system with a heat exchanger unit like that of a car, whereas a sterndrive uses water from the lake, river or sea for cooling and has its own impeller.)

1 Drain off water from the engine coolant system and replace with anti-freeze solution as recommended.

2 Mix a strong solution of correct anti-freeze with fresh water and, using a hose attached to the lower leg water intake, run up the engine at idling speed to circulate the mixture. Stop the engine and remove the impeller.

3 Unscrew each of the fuel injectors and add to each cylinder about a teaspoon of the recommended anti-corrosion oil.

4 De-gunk the engine and transmission and wash everything down with a solution of soap-based washing-up liquid (not detergent). All the dirt and waste will fall into the engine compartment.

5 Thoroughly clean the engine compartment. This is a difficult job, but one well worth doing. Use a rag, sponges, de-gunk, washing-up liquid and fresh water until it is polished and shiny. This work will pay dividends when you come to sell or exchange your boat.

6 Dry off and coat or spray with marine water displacement oil for total protection. Lubricate all the cables and linkages.

7 Remove the battery, run it flat and store it in a warm, dry place. If you disconnected the hose to the impeller pump on the sterndrive, reassemble it now.

### Recommissioning

1 Put in a fully-charged battery.

2 Drain the anti-corrosion oil and replace with the recommended engine oil.

3 Re-install the water pump impeller to the stern drive.

4 Remove the fuel injectors and crank over the engine several times to remove excess oil from the cylinders. Replace the injectors.

5 Replace fuel filter and fill the tank with fresh diesel fuel.

6 Check all lines and connections, and check that all seacocks and bungs are in position.

7 Lower the craft into the water, open the outside water valve and check all the connections for leaks. Run the engine as soon as possible. If the engine turns over but does not fire properly, there could be air in the fuel system. See the section on bleeding a diesel fuel system in Chapter 12.

## HULL MAINTENANCE: RIGID HULLS

Today the vast majority of rigid powerboat hulls are made of glass reinforced plastic or GRP (commonly known as glassfibre). This requires very little work to maintain it in good condition.

Hose down the hull with fresh water after every session, and wash down with a bio-degradable washing-up liquid in warm water at least twice a year. Use glassfibre cleaner to remove obstinate grease marks, and polish with a non-silicone polish at least once a year.

Small surface scratches can be eliminated using fine wet-and-dry sandpaper, a rubbing compound and polish. Deeper scores will need repairing with epoxy filler: undercut the edges of the gouge and clean it out with acetone before applying the filler. Overfill slightly and allow 24 hours to cure. Then rub down as above.

Major damage is best repaired professionally in case the strength of the hull has been compromised.

## HULL MAINTENANCE: INFLATABLES

The advanced construction methods used for manufacturing inflatables and semi-rigid inflatables ensures long life and reliability, but they must be well cared for. Make sure you hose down with fresh water each time the boat is used.

➤ **A periodic application of non-silicone polish will keep GRP clean and bright, and will help the boat maintain its resale value.**